To Heal
the Earth

To Heal
the Earth

A Theology of Ecology

■

Frederick
Quinn

UPPER
ROOM BOOKS
NASHVILLE

Cover photo: John Netherton
First printing: March 1994 (5)
ISBN: 0-8358-0702-9
Library of Congress Catalog Card Number: 93-60146

Printed in the United States of America

For Alison and Christopher

And all the trees of the field shall clap their hands.

ॐ Isaiah 55:12, NRSV

Riddle # 66: Creation

I am greater than all this world, smaller
Than the smallest worm; I walk more softly
Than the moon, swifter than the sun. I hold
Oceans and seas in my arms; the earth's
Green fields lie on my breast. I touch
Endless depths, deeper than hell,
And reach higher than Heaven, further than
The stars and the angels' home. I fill
The earth, the world, and its rushing waters
With myself. Say my name, if you know it.

෭ *Poems from the Old English*
Burton Raffel, translator

Contents

Preface

*O*NE EASTER SATURDAY *I* WENT TO THE CIRCUS. *Inside the dark tent animals, acrobats, and clowns pointed toward the center ring. Drums rolled and spotlights crisscrossed rapidly.*

High in the center ring, a mirrored globe turned slowly. On it stood a drugged tiger. At the crack of the ringmaster's whip, the tiger stretched as upright as a four-legged creature can, extended its paws as if on a cross, straddling the spangled world. The obviously sedated creature kept its balance and dignity.

Words from the Good Friday liturgy returned through the whooped-up applause and metallic arpeggio: If I be lifted up, I will draw all persons unto me.

Christ the Tiger, pray for me, *I thought as the majestic animal descended from the globe and strode purposefully toward the dark cage. Good Friday and Easter, the climax of the liturgical year, reflect the presence of Christ in all creation. The desolation of Good Friday and the renewal of life at Easter are for all nature, which includes both humanity and the biosphere.*

I HAVE BEEN WRITING SOME OF THIS BOOK since childhood. The changes of the seasons, an awareness of plant and animal life and of links between the liturgical and calendar years were natural for a child growing up in rural Pennsylvania. In college I read Paul Tillich's sermon, "Nature, Also, Mourns for a Lost Good," and I knew its ideas would trigger a response someday. A series of epiphanies described in this text linked religion and nature for me.

Events coalesced in the early 1990s. I attended the Second World Climate Conference in Geneva and chaired the Environment Committee of the Episcopal Diocese of Washington. Scientific, public policy, and religious issues converged with requests to write and speak. I do so from an Anglican perspective, combining scripture, tradition, and reason. At its best, this viewpoint gives due weight to both scientific and religious arguments, which is necessary in understanding contemporary ecological problems and in suggesting solutions.

As always, faith leads to action. Excellent local, national, and international environmental groups can provide support for individuals and communities in this common cause. We cannot avoid decisions. We may never obtain all the information we want on some questions, but at some point we have enough information to decide on a course of action. Such information is available to us now on many ecological questions.

For me, the most compelling aspect of the environmental issue is its intergenerational dimension. Humanity's decisions in the immediate years ahead will have consequences for a rising and yet-to-be-born generation. I remember the African proverb:

> *Treat the earth well. It was not given to you by your parents. It was loaned to you by your children.*

∾ Frederick Quinn

Acknowledgments

I GRATEFULLY ACKNOWLEDGE THE CONTRIBUTION, through conversations or letters, of A. M. Allchin, Carla Berkedal, Daniel B. Botkin, Frederick Buechner, Frank B. Cervany, Thomas M. Chappell, Susan Fisher, Harold Graves, Michael P. Hamilton, Carolyn Tanner Irish, Charles H. Long, Thomas E. Lovejoy, Joan Martin-Brown, Henry and Virginia Mitchell, James Parks Morton, Evelina Moulder, G. O. P. Obasi, Martin Palmer, Charles P. Price, Ann Reeder, Lee Talbot, Russell E. Train, Charlotte Quinn, Samuel Van Culin, and Erica Wood.

Introduction

Grandfather, look on our brokenness.
We know that in all creation only the human family
has strayed from the Sacred Way. . . .
Grandfather, Sacred One, teach us love, compassion, and honour,
that we may heal the earth and heal each other.

        A prayer of the Ojibway people of Canada[1]

T HE ENVIRONMENTAL CRISIS IS NOW PART of the discourse of politicians, scientists, business leaders, and ordinary citizens. In analyzing the crisis, we all bring different perspectives. One approach is to adopt the framework that biblical writers used when wrestling with fundamental questions about humanity, its relationship to the world and to the Creator, Sustainer, and Redeemer of life. This perspective allows us to grasp the problem and to shape our response. Scientists may argue that data is inadequate; politicians can suggest that public policy choices are not evident. A religious response will not provide the missing numbers or distinct legislative prescriptions, but it will suggest a framework from which all parties may view the problem. This response differs from that of the Victorian who, when informed of Charles Darwin's theories of evolution, replied, "I hope they are not true . . . and if they are, I hope people will have the decency not to talk about them in public."

We are into new waters here. Most scientists concede that environmental problems have no simple, quick-fix solutions. The scientific findings' incompleteness, the solutions' staggering costs, and the problem's planetary dimensions frustrate public officials. The issue is about life on a local and global scale; the preservation of species, including humanity; and our direct role in caring for the universe God entrusted to us.

Recently, an international gathering of scientists and religious leaders made the following statement: "As scientists, many of us have had profound experiences of awe and reverence before the universe. We understand that what is regarded as sacred is more likely to be treated with care and respect. Our planetary home should be so regarded."[2] A Methodist statement suggests the issue's global dimensions: "Our planet is the setting for a great range of beings to live in inter-dependence with each other, with the elements and with the non-sentient forms of life. The earth itself depends upon sun and moon, stars and galaxies. Upon it birds and fish, animals and insects depend upon sun, air and water, plants and each other, and are constantly changing in form. No one form of life has absolute value or permanence."[3]

Faith leads to action. Now is the time for religiously concerned people of this generation to meld scientific data and religious faith, to interpret ancient biblical passages about reverence for creation in light of present-day problems. Religious bodies, individuals, and larger communities must turn from self-willed destruction of creation to a balanced use of the universe God has placed in our care. Such a viewpoint will not answer the question of global warming or ozone layer depletion. It will not calculate the ideal number of elephants for Africa or buffalo for America but will help us understand the deep affinity between people and other creatures, an affinity illustrated in the Buddhist poem:

> *Come back, O Tigers! to the woods again,*
> *And let it not be levelled with the plain;*

For, without you, the axe will lay it low;
You, without it, for ever homeless go.[4]

Judeo-Christian belief sees a unity in all nature created by God. We often interpret such unity as a hierarchy with vertical layers of power, starting with God, followed by humanity, then animals, and then the world. We often have interpreted the creation story to mean hierarchical and patriarchal dominion. While hierarchy and patriarchy were features of traditional Hebrew society, their biblical meaning goes well beyond accepted cultural concepts of that time. The Hebrew God was neither male nor female, unlike deities of Canaanite religion. The Hebrew word *bara'* means "create," but God is the verb's subject. Only God can create, and the energy of God's creative act extends to all aspects of the universe.

For some Christians, the Genesis stories are scientific documents, lacking only supporting mathematical tables; for others, they are a statement of who made the world, not how it was made. In past centuries, a passionate debate raged between traditional biblical commentators and scientists. But in recent times, events have overcome old divisions. In modern environmental studies, scientists and theologians are allies, driven by mutual concern over our planet's destruction.

I believe that the environmental crisis requires a religiously-informed response. Such a response is available through the Bible but not in traditionally accepted ways. Many contemporary Christians confine creation theology to a few selected passages from Genesis, often interpreted out of context. The demands of the ecological crisis that humanity has created force us to rethink our religious understanding of creation. Approaching this problem from a different angle, a well-known environmental scientist, Daniel B. Botkin writes,

Accepting the premises for a new religious perspective, the next step is to reread the Bible. Some supposedly familiar passages will take on strikingly new and different meaning. Dominion might mean control in the way a pilot controls an aircraft, but neither invented the aircraft nor plans to alter it beyond its functioning state. To love people means to want to continue to live on Earth, and to work for the system that supports their living also to continue. A loving God does not wish to have the system that sustains life destroyed; there is no conflict between the biosphere's functioning and the dictates of such a God. In fact, if a loving God's primal act is the creation of heaven and earth, then humanity must acknowledge a symbiotic relationship among creation's parts, which include the biosphere with its numerous ecosystems. Humanity's mandate is thus to work within the whole of creation to preserve and enhance its life-sustaining possibilities now and for future generations.[5]

Reading the environmentally related passages of the Old and New Testaments suggests possibilities for common cause of science and religion, especially when we place the nature sections of the psalms and the Pauline creation hymns in context. Here is a world of cosmic order in which creation throbs and humankind is free to choose redemptive or destructive paths; a world that juxtaposes violent storms, fires, and volcanoes with silent growth, the intricate web of marshlands, and rain forests. Destructive earth-moving machines work alongside vulnerable birds and mammals. Chaos and creation compete. An ancient Easter hymn says, "Death and life have contended in that combat stupendous."

Notes

1. George Appleton, gen. ed., *The Oxford Book of Prayer* (New York: Oxford University Press, 1985), 25.

2. "Preserving and Cherishing the Earth," *Christianity and Crisis*, Vol. 50, No. 7, 14 May 1990, 143.

3. "A Discussion Document on Christian Faith Concerning the Environment," *Floods and Rainbows: A Study Guide on the Environment—for Those who Care about the Future* (Methodist Church Division of Social Responsibility: London, 1991).

4. From the Jataka stories, quoted by Martin Palmer, *Creation Festival Liturgy* (Manchester: ICOREC, 1988), 33.

5. Daniel B. Botkin and Frederick Quinn, "The Uneasy Alliance: Religion, Science and the Environment," ms., Washington, D.C., 1992, 18.

Part I

The Bible and Ecology

One

The Old Testament

*A*UNT HAZEL TAUGHT SUNDAY SCHOOL *at the Rocky Grove Presbyterian Church, and I first learned about dominion and covenant from her. I was ten years old. Aunt Hazel had advance access to children's Sunday school materials, including the all-important teacher's guide, which I scanned before Sunday school to see where the flannelgraphs, sandbox villages, hand puppets, and coloring sheets were leading.*

The Sunday school room was painted ivory—the color of Aunt Hazel's kitchen, which was the color of choice in Rocky Grove in those years. The walls displayed neatly placed biblical illustrations, including a parchment-like scroll that resembled a high school diploma, over which the word covenant *appeared in a local approximation of Gothic script. On another wall next to a window that opened on the Volunteer Fire Department's building was a rainbow. Elsewhere, a class several years ago had painted a large mural of Noah's ark, with two of every animal, illustrated from pictures provided by the Pennsylvania Department of Agriculture's Home Extension Service.*

Aunt Hazel stood before the class in sensible brown teacher's shoes and explained the concepts of covenant and dominion to class members whose lives were not far from the soil, coming as they did from nearby farms or small houses with large kitchen gardens. Covenant was the basic relationship between God and humanity. If people behaved, they could then claim dominion over the earth. Everything was there for our unrestricted but prudent use. The message of Noah and the Flood was that humanity's playing God got most of the human race drowned; but if we were good, nature's golden garden was there for the picking.

A clear statement of our responsibility as stewards completed the picture. Aunt Hazel described the steward as someone not unlike an attendant at the Arlington Hotel or a hired hand on a farm—someone who worked hard, watched the master's possessions, asked no questions, and took no initiatives. The master was like the olive-skinned, hirsute young man pictured as "The Master" on the Lake D. Steffee Funeral Home fans used widely in Venango County churches before air-conditioning. For rural people growing up in the American heartland, covenant, dominion, and stewardship fit together in an easily accessible package. They were as much a part of the local culture as Arrow shirts, Model T cars, and the Sears and Roebuck catalog.

THESE IDEAS WERE AS SIMPLE AS THEY WERE INCOMPLETE; I was an adult before I could sort them out. Often popular theology is little more than Sunday school beliefs amplified with statistics. Sometimes we confront the ecological crisis with outdated concepts and unexamined religious beliefs that do not serve us well in the time ahead.

Sin: Against God and God's Creation

What standards should guide us in this complex debate? How can we approach the issue personally? Reexamining the idea of sin can restore an ethical agenda to the environment, pointing the way to humanity's restoration of its relationship with a loving, merciful God, the giver of life and the earth's gifts. God loves all categories of creation; all come from God, relate actively to one another, and return eventually to God. That is the meaning of doxology when linked to creation.

Sin distorts this relationship. Sin includes both a willful turning away from God and the systematic destruction of God's creation. Sin can also be distortion of good intentions. The Greek word for sin, *hamartia*, came from an archery term meaning "to miss the mark."

> [We] have become the greatest abusers of the earth, exploiting it with selfish carelessness and adopting an attitude of ruthless arrogance towards nature. That attitude, at the core of our sinfulness, is closely linked to our fear and envy towards each other, to the injustice and hatred which poison human relationships, and thus to our disobedience towards God. The whole created order had been infected with evil.[1]

Sin exists both personally and communally; it includes individual actions and the activity of power concentrated in corporations, governments, and churches. There are sins of omission and commission. Our actions destroy the ozone layer; our inaction allows the destruction of biodiversity around us—both are equally sinful acts. An often-stated formulation is this: "We have left undone those things which we ought to have done, and we have done those things which we ought not to have done."[2] An older version added, "And there is no health in us," an apt image of ecological devastation. The plea is for restoration.

What constitutes sin in a specifically ecological context? Sin involves putting immediate human drives and desires for satisfaction at the forefront of existence. Examples include wasting or consuming excessive food, energy, and natural resources. Another example is hardness of heart toward the silent voices of nature and the host of inarticulate creatures comprising the ecosystem. The writer of the Letter of Jude describes the results of human ecological sin: "They are shepherds who take care only of themselves. They are clouds carried along by a wind without giving rain, trees fruitless in autumn, dead twice over and pulled up by the roots. They are wild sea waves, foaming with disgraceful deeds; they are stars that have wandered from their courses, and the place reserved for them is an eternity of blackest darkness" (Jude 12-13).

Sin is the opposite of cherishing creation. Sin is putting a person, a group of people, or a nation in the place of God; thereby creating lunar landscapes of pollution and destruction. Veiling the sun with industrial smoke and filling the heavens with chlorofluorocarbons is a conscious decision. In satisfying human desires and needs, we destroy habitat and leave our posterity a crippled world. Archbishop Michael Peers, Primate, Anglican Church of Canada, described environmental sin as:

> Not simply human greed, nor is it even blindness and indifference to our neighbors, though in truth these are bad enough. At its deepest level it is rebellion against God as source and mystery of all created life, and our wilful misuse of God's creation. We are in danger of fulfilling an ancient and terrible biblical warning, one that many of us thought was primitive and outdated, that of visiting the sins of the parents upon the children and their children's children. It is a prophecy being fulfilled in our own lifetime. God's justice therefore calls us to repentance and fundamental change.[3]

Thus sin has multiple meanings. Sin exists actively and passively, individually and corporately. In describing the human condition, Emmanuel Kant once wrote, "Out of the crooked timber of humanity no straight thing was ever made." Isaiah depicts the human predicament in prophetic language:

> The earth dries up and withers,
>> The world languishes and withers; . . .
> The earth lies polluted under its inhabitants. . . .
>> All joy has reached its eventide (24:4, 5, 11, NRSV).

Aldo Leopold's environmental masterpiece, *A Sand County Almanac*, contains a profound description of sin and an understanding of sin's impact on creation. The well-known naturalist describes the deep affinity between wolves and mountains, and how, through a devastating event, he came to appreciate that relationship:

> My own conviction on this score dates from the day I saw a wolf die. We were eating lunch on a high rimrock, at the foot of which a turbulent river elbowed its way. We saw what we thought was a doe fording the torrent, her breast awash in white water. When she climbed the bank toward us and shook out her tail, we realized our error: it was a wolf. A half-dozen others, evidently grown pups, sprang from the willows and all joined in a welcoming mêlée of wagging tails and playful maulings. What was literally a pile of wolves writhed and tumbled in the center of an open flat at the foot of our rimrock.
>
> In those days we had never heard of passing up a chance to kill a wolf. In a second we were pumping lead into the pack, but with more excitement than accuracy: how to aim a steep downhill shot is always confusing. When our rifles were empty, the old wolf was down, and a pup was dragging a leg into impassable slide-rocks.
>
> We reached the old wolf in time to watch a fierce green fire dying in her eyes. I realized then, and have known ever since, that there was something new to me in those eyes—something known only to her and to the mountain. I was young then, and full of trigger-itch. I thought that because fewer wolves meant more deer, that no wolves would mean hunters' paradise. But after seeing the green fire die, I sensed that neither the wolf nor the mountain agreed with such a view.[4]

Our biblical heritage as Christians provides profound descriptions of sin, as well as graphic depictions of sin's impact on creation.

Biblical accounts offer images both of paradise and of a broken and fragmented world.

Genesis: In the Beginning

The Genesis narratives bear examination. Genesis 1:1–2:3 and Genesis 2:4-25 are two distinctly different creation accounts by separate authors, to which later material was appended. In the first account, written around 450 B.C., God created both women and men. In the second account, written around 950 B.C., God created woman after man. Genesis 1:1–2:3 emphasizes the cosmos and humanity's place in it; Genesis 2:4-25 restricts the setting to the Garden of Eden. The first creation story opens with the words: *In the beginning God created the heavens and the earth.* Lofty passages about creation's seven days describe the spirit of God moving over the face of the waters; God's creating light, dividing the light from the darkness; making firmament, heaven, earth, growing things—fruit trees and seed; lights in the firmament to separate day and night, sun and moon, stars; waters swarming with living things, great sea-beasts and birds.

Then God says, "Let the earth bring forth living creatures, according to their various kinds: cattle, creeping things, and wild animals, all according to their various kinds" (1:24). Next God says, "'Let us make human beings in our image, after our likeness, to have dominion over the fish in the sea, the birds of the air, the cattle, all wild animals on land, and everything that creeps on the earth.' God created human beings in his own image; in the image of God he created them; male and female he created them" (1:26-27).

The Paradise story (Gen. 2:4–3:24) has a tighter focus. It centers on humanity's will to rebel. The Garden of Eden is not an isolated park, as often envisioned, but the setting of human rebellion. Genesis 1:1–2:3 is about creation, all of which God saw as good. Beginning with Genesis 2:4, the scene narrows to the earth; Adam is of the earth, consigned to till the soil, and destined to return to it at death. From a contemporary ecological perspective, this creation story pictures humanity's struggle for redemption in the lands east of Eden.

Often humanity has interpreted, "Be fruitful and increase, fill the earth and subdue it, have dominion over . . . every living thing" (Gen. 1:28) as its marching orders to exploit the universe. But the biblical message, when considered in historic and social context, is that humans and animals should live from the fruits of the earth as produced by plants and trees. To "subdue" was to till or cultivate the land, not conquer and control every corner of it. The injunction to "be fruitful and increase" came at a time when the Hebrew population was small, and land was plentiful. We cannot consider this order to be a timeless biblical mandate for unrestricted population growth or a command that must continue in today's world. The words *fruitful*, meaning fertile, and *increase* are contradictory in contemporary society. We live on a planet of limited resources and population-carrying capacity. The goals of steady population increase and augmenting peoples' quality of life, including access to food, health care, education, and economic advancement, are on a collision course. Obeying the second injunction creates conditions in which the first is unrealizable. Genesis 1:28 is a primordial blessing—a minor, dated passage—in a more complex story.

The Genesis accounts are not factual science or history but interpretative explanations of God's presence and relation to the world. Metaphor and imagery communicate the faith community's understanding of its history. Humanity still wrestles with the deep questions that biblical writers raise about human conduct in light of God's presence and purposes.

Genesis: Dominion and Covenant

When we interpret these opening chapters of Genesis as making humanity the center or epitome of creation, with all else as subservient, we fall into dangerous reasoning. We begin to think that God created all things to meet our every desire. We begin to think that the world exists for our sake to satisfy our own ends, to be used or destroyed for our benefit. Such theology interprets creation as an endlessly supplied supermarket or shopping mall that provides for humanity's needs and desires while asking little in return.

Few biblical words have raised more controversy in their interpretion than the words *dominion* and *covenant*. People have used both to sanction the exploitation of the universe, although the biblical message about the proper use of creation is far more comprehensive than these words suggest. As legal terms, *dominion* and *covenant* had restricted meaning, essentially of a superior party and inferior client relationship. In the ancient Middle East, a ruler had dominion, life and death power, over subjects; but power was tempered with a mandate to govern wisely and use resources prudently for the benefit of all.

Modern biblical commentators employ a broader concept of dominion and covenant. Several scholars understand the basic biblical covenant as a relationship not only between God and Israel but between God and all creation. Humanity's role is only part of creation. This understanding is a profound shift from earlier interpretations about covenant. In Genesis 9, Noah's covenant is mutually supportive and accountable with the whole of creation. We can read the covenant language in the opening chapters of Genesis as a covenant between God and the whole of creation also.

David Trickett, a Methodist scholar, states, "The question now is: who is the other party? Covenant is a very rich and broad concept, as is dominion. We are used to thinking of relationships of superiority or inferiority, but that is a dangerous vision. Accountability has to go both ways."[5]

Many modern-day biblical scholars, such as Claus Westermann and Ian Bradley, reject the idea of dominion over nature as exploitation. An international environmental lawyer, Edith Brown Weiss, argues that covenant and dominion should include specific enforceable planetary rights: "Each generation is both a trustee or custodian of the planet for future generations and a beneficiary of previous generations' stewardship. This circumstance imposes certain obligations on us to care for our legacy just as it gives us certain rights to use the legacy."[6] The purpose of intergenerational equity is for all countries to pass on the planet in no worse condition than the generation received it. This idea conforms with the intergenerational nature of biblical covenants, as in God's covenant with Noah, which is with "you and . . . your offspring forever" (Gen. 13:15, NRSV).

An Arizona trial lawyer and naturalist, George L. Paul, asked, "Do we have fiduciary duties for all those silent creatures that create life on earth? We are the caretaker species for the whole planet. We are not just the only creatures on the planet that have a right to exist and be free from pain. Much of the diversity of life could be wiped out in the next 150 years. All this diversity is there to give our ecosystem support."[7]

Dominion and covenant are not the only, nor the most important, concepts about creation in the Old Testament. Western biblical interpretations have seized on them as justification for exploiting the earth and its resources. Scripture accounts of creation, especially the Book of Job, the Song of the Three, and the Psalms, as well as Genesis and Isaiah, portray a more complex world. Their portrayal comes closer to the world modern scientists know: a place filled with both contradictions and hope. This portrayal provides both a more accurate picture of creation in its biblical context and a road map to help us navigate through the present ecological danger.

Genesis: The Ark and the Flood

The *nave* of a church means "boat," and those who sit in the nave are like boat people. I thought of this during an Easter vigil service at a historic downtown Washington, D.C., church, the Church of the Epiphany. A predawn wind sprang up, causing the high wooden roofbeams to creak like ship's timbers in a storm. The building's interior architectural lines resembled a nineteenth-century wooden ship. Meanwhile, the small congregation, like passengers on a modern-day Noah's ark, huddled inside by candlelight, oblivious to wind and rain, to hear the creation and resurrection accounts of life's springing from darkness.

For centuries, humanity separated creation from nature, allowing the earth to be exploited freely. Today, humanity returns increasingly to a biblical view of nature as God's creation, to be respected and cherished as such. God both creates the world and, at the same time, enters into it.

The account of Noah's ark and the great Flood (Gen. 6:9–9:17) restates themes of the Paradise story. Here again, we read of divine judgment in history. While god-and-flood stories abound in the riverine cultures of the Fertile Crescent, this one is different. God provides humanity with a redemptive way. Noah finds favor with God. His family members take pairs of each animal with them into the ark, and God saves them all. The account ends with the restoration of nature, "seedtime and harvest, cold and heat, summer and winter, day and night" (8:22). God vows to never strike the earth again with such judgment despite humanity's evil inclinations. The contemporary challenge to the children of God is to leave the world similarly intact.

God establishes a covenant with Noah following the flood: "My bow I set in the clouds to be a sign of the covenant between myself and the earth" (Gen. 9:13). The covenant was a pact between a superior party, God, and a lesser vassal, Noah. It enumerated each one's obligations. God brings Noah safely to dry land, while promising never to destroy life by such a flood again. In a modern environmental context, we can understand the covenant as being between God and all living creatures, broadening the base of participating parties. Noah is a trustee on behalf of all creation. The rainbow is a permanent reminder of the lasting covenant between God and creation.

Elijah and Nature: "A Cloud Coming up from the West"

"I see a cloud no bigger than a man's hand, coming up from the west." Elijah the prophet kneels on top of Mount Carmel with his servant. Israel endures a prolonged drought, and Elijah feuds with the local rainmakers. He sends word to Ahab, the ruler, "to harness his chariot and be off, or the rain will stop him." Soon "the sky grew black with clouds, the wind rose, and heavy rain began to fall." (See 1 Kings 18:41-46.)

Possibly a ninth century B.C. author interspersed the Elijah stories into 1 Kings 17–19. They are interpretations of history rather than factual accounts, representing a consistent Old Testament message: Yahweh's authority over the land's fertility and God's presence in nature. The location shifts from the Garden of Eden to a drought-plagued land. The contest is between Yahweh's representative and the local Baal worshipers and their scattered regional gods. The story and the drought ends with the sound of rushing rain. Biblical writers frequently used storms, fire, and thunder to dramatically announce the presence of Yahweh. These disturbances call attention to events beyond the natural. Today droughts, storms, sea rise, and global warming cause contemporary people to ask, "Is there a divine message here about the way we treat the universe? When God announces to disobedient Israelites that their excesses will result in floods, earthquakes, and fire, could that message possibly have relevance to us?"

Job: The Voice from the Tempest
Toward the end of the Book of Job, we find a significant, but often ignored, creation account. In striking language, the narrative describes both God's relationship with humanity and God's continual presence in creation.

The basic question in Job is the relationship of humanity to God, but the author interprets Yahweh's tie with creation in equally powerful language. The voice from the tempest raises questions that do not answer Job's queries but make them insignificant before a merciful Creator. (See Job 38–41.)

> Where were you when I laid the
> earth's foundations?
> . . . .
> Who set its corner-stone in place,
>   while the morning stars sang in chorus
> And the [heavenly beings] shouted for joy? (38:4, 6-7)

Hearing these chapters read aloud is like listening to a Bach fugue. Themes build and are restated; delicate colorings appear between lines, magnifying main themes. Unquestionably, the whole is more than the sum of its parts.

The creation passages describe order in the earth's movement despite the presence of discordant chaos:

> Who supported the sea at its birth,
>   when it burst in flood from the womb—
> when I wrapped it in a blanket of cloud
>   and swaddled it in dense fog,
> when I established its bounds,
>   set its barred doors in place,
> and said, "Thus far may you come
>   but no farther;
> here your surging waves must halt"? (38:8-11)

And, in contrast, consider this passage of Audubon-like detail:

> Do you instruct the eagle to soar aloft
>   and build its nest high up?
> It dwells among the rocks and there
>   it has its nest,
>   secure on a rocky crag;
> from there it searches for food,
>   keenly scanning the distance,
> that its brood may be gorged with blood;
>   wherever the slain are, it is there. (39:27-30)

The nature chapters in Job contrast with the more peaceful creation story in Genesis 1:1–2:4. In Job, God keeps a potentially violent, disruptive nature in bounds. The world of Job more closely resembles our own than that of Genesis. God asks Job these questions:

> Have you visited the storehouses of
>   the snow

or seen the arsenal where hail is
stored,
which I have kept ready for the day
of calamity,
for war and for the hour of battle? (38:22-23)

Job 39 contains five sets of poetic images. The first is of animals'
giving birth, the second of obstreperous wild asses and oxen, the
third of an ostrich that leaves its eggs unprotected in the sand and
"treats her chicks heartlessly as if they were not her own, . . . while
like a cock she struts over the uplands, scorning both horse and
rider" (39:16, 18).

The fourth image is that of the strong horse ready for battle
who "quiver[s] like a locust's wings, when his shrill neighing strikes
terror." The final shorter section (39:26-30) is of hawks and eagles.

Within a short verbal frieze, Job's author depicts God as
nature's sovereign. Yahweh's established parameters contain the
primal element's energy. Job is an account, not of victory over
human suffering and natural disorder, but of Job's faith in spite of
suffering and of God's presence in an unruly universe. The Book of
Job's literary power helps humanity glimpse both the omnipotent
creator of the universe at work and an omnipresent God hovering
over the universe's most minute corners and crevices.

The Song of the Three
God's Continual Presence in Creation

The most encompassing Old Testament statement of God's continual presence in creation is The Song of the Three, an addition to
Daniel that we find in the Greek version of the Old Testament. This
lengthy poem is the song three youths sing in the fiery furnace. It is
among the most ordered biblical descriptions of creation, yet it
gives full measure as well to nature's random, capricious side.

Nebuchadnezzar tells the youths to renounce Yahweh while
the king's servants feed the fire in the furnace. The fire consumes
several nearby Chaldaeans, and then the angel of the Lord scatters
the flames, and the three are unharmed. An extended hymn of praise

to Yahweh follows, in which the three call upon all creation to bless the Lord. Creation includes the heavens, waters above the heavens, sun and moon, winds that blast, sleet and falling snow. Mountains and hills, growing things, flowing springs, seas and rivers, whales and aquatic life, birds, cattle and wild beasts praise Yahweh. The Song has two conclusions: All nature praises God; and humanity is part of creation, not its central force.

The Oxford Cycle of Prayer extends The Song over a month of daily readings. During this time, I was in Geneva for a United Nations meeting of diplomats, scientists, and environmentalists who were discussing global climate change. Their findings were that earth's temperatures are warming more quickly than at any time in the past 10,000 years. Unless we reduce greenhouse gas emissions, average temperatures may rise by up to 3°C within a century. The world will experience a likely sea rise of 65 centimeters by the next century's end if "business as usual" conditions prevail.

As the slow cog train headed for the Matterhorn range, I read both the scientific research documents and the biblical passage. "If sea level rise affects only one percent of the projected global population of six billion by the year 2000, then global warming will have created 60 million more environmental victims, environmental refugees."[8] I read alternately from the scientific documents and The Song:

> *Let the whole creation bless the Lord, sing his praise and exalt him for ever.*
> Increasing drought risk represents potentially the most serious impact of climate change on agriculture regionally and globally.
>
> *Bless the Lord, all rain and dew . . . . all winds that blow.*
> Rapid sea-level rise would change coastal ecology and threaten many important fisheries. Reductions in sea ice will benefit shipping, but seriously impact on ice-dependent marine mammals and birds.

Bless the Lord, fire and heat . . . . searing blast and bitter cold.

With an increase in mean temperature, episodes of high temperature will most likely become more frequent in the future, and cold periods less frequent; increased incidence of disturbances such as pest outbreaks and forest fires are likely.

Biblical images and scientific statements intermingled as the late afternoon wind brought bone-chilling cold from the Alps. I headed toward the village below, trying to reconcile the two worldviews.

A bronze church bell rang through the autumn air. Following the sound, I sat wearily in the back pew of Zermatt's rococo church. My eyes followed the predictable ornamentation to the discovery of a tastefully executed contemporary ceiling mural of Noah's ark. A Swiss Noah held an alpine bird at the mural's center. The Alps were the ark's landfall. A mountain bear, goat, horse, elephant, and kangaroo looked on. The ark was of rural carpentry construction; its inhabitants were Swiss villagers surrounded by tropical animals. Consigned to the dark ocean depths were polluting smokestacks, demonic sharks, Adam and Eve, and a skeletal figure peering from a TV screen.

The Zermatt railway station displayed a poster for an exhibition in Geneva's Palais des Nations, "War and Peace, from a Century of War to a Century of Hope." Beneath the color photo of Planet Earth shot from space was a Kenyan proverb: "Treat the earth well. It was not given to you by your parents. It was loaned to you by your children."

Bible passages like The Song of the Three and the story of Noah's ark confront a world problem with a religious message. Older definitions of covenant and dominion will not hold. Earth and the biosphere are not passive participants in creation but alive and intricate, to be cherished by humanity as a divine gift. Humans are part of the splendor of creation, but we risk destroying it.

Confronted with a problem, part of our response is to realize the incompleteness of our first reading of the Bible on this central issue.

The Psalms: Discordant Harmony

Many people believe nature behaves like a bucolic scene in a nineteenth-century landscape, such as Edward Hicks's "Peaceable Kingdom." They assume a world of ordered vistas, benign animals, and irenic, hard-working farmers. In reality, nature contains violence and contradictions as well as basic order. It is a world the psalm writers understood. A contemporary biologist and environmentalist, Daniel B. Botkin, has studied the evolution of numerous forests and animal species carefully. He believes that complexity, chance, simultaneity of events, history, and changes are the qualities of nature. Nature is not a gentle, ordered, harmonious process, but a patchwork of intricate systems within which many things happen at once. Each system undergoes changes at different rates of time and space. It would seem that chance plays an important role.

Scientists are only beginning to comprehend natural change; in the evolving discipline of chaos theory, computer graphics display patterns of symmetry and beauty in the presence of apparent disorder. The psalms, considered in their entirety, depict such a world. It is possible to construct a scientific and biblical viewpoint of nature as an open, evolving, and often contradictory process. The psalms describe order and disorder; they address the random and capricious side of human behavior and nature, as well as the beautiful and harmonious.

Readers will find idyllic God-in-nature passages in the psalms. But reading the psalms closely reveals the discordant harmonies that Botkin describes. Consider the nature passages in Psalm 74, a communal lament:

> By your power you cleft the sea monster in two
> and broke the sea serpent's heads in the waters;
> . . . .
> You opened channels for spring and torrent;

> you dried up streams never known to fail.
> The day is yours, yours also is the night;
>   you ordered the light of moon and sun.
> You have fixed all the regions of the earth;
>   you created both summer and winter.
> . . . .
> Look upon your creatures: they are
>   filled with dark thoughts,
> and the land is a haunt of violence.
> —Psalm 74:13, 15-17, 20

In short, nature has a dark and unpredictable side: forests burn, earthquakes and volcanoes alter landscapes, locust plagues darken the sun. God remains the righteous force above and within it all, not a kindly circus master producing only happy acts or the detached inventor of a mechanistic universe. The Hebrew God is providential and generous, asking in return, not self-absorption but praise. In Psalm 78 God feeds the starving, wandering Israelites on the Exodus journey:

> [God] let loose the east wind from heaven
>   and drove the south wind by his power;
> [God] rained meat down on them like a dust storm,
>   birds flying thick as the sand of the seashore.
> He made them fall within the camp,
>   all around their tents. (vv. 26-28)

The psalmist's perspective is that of a people liberated from bondage, praising God, and realistically describing the heights and depths of human experience. The people are seeking shalom, wholeness, and unity with God and God's creation. In Psalm 8, the writer asks God this question:

> What are human beings that you
>   are mindful of them,
> mortals that you care for them? (v. 4, NRSV)

Human beings have power to harness and control creation; God has "given them dominion over the works of [God's] hands" (Ps. 8:6, NRSV). However, humanity's place is as part of creation, not as the only actor. A contemporary theologian, commenting on Psalm 104, says the psalmist places humans "with great artistry, in the context of all the other teeming life on the earth. Nothing is done to highlight [them]: [they are] just . . . other figure[s] in the landscape."[9] We can accept the idea of humanity's role as the apex of creation, but we often confuse that idea with a license for wanton exploitation. The Hebrew word for dominion is *'abad*, meaning "to till and serve the land." The word for exploitation is *shamar*, meaning "to keep" the earth. By returning to the biblical picture of humanity and its relationship to creation, we will rediscover something rural people have known all along: the deep ties among God, people, and the earth. Much of our journey is just going home and finding what was there all along.

The Bible's five last psalms provide a framework for praising God and thus finding a new meaning in creation:

> Great is the LORD and most worthy of praise;
> his greatness is beyond all searching out.
>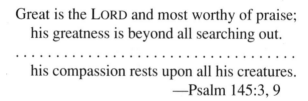
> his compassion rests upon all his creatures.
> —Psalm 145:3, 9

In language suggestive of the Magnificat, the psalmist includes issues of justice and equity in the relationship of creation to God: "The LORD supports all who stumble and raises all who are bowed down" (Ps. 145:14). All creation depends on the Creator for sustenance:

> All raise their eyes to you in hope,
> and you give them their food when
> it is due.
> You open your hand
> and satisfy every living creature with
> your favour.
> —Psalm 145:15-16

God is active in all creation and is the subject of praise from God's creatures. The categories resemble those in Genesis and Job, including "wild animals and all cattle; creeping creatures and winged birds. . . . princes and rulers over the whole earth" (148:10, 11). The final injunction is this: "Let everything that has breath praise the LORD!" (150:6)

The Psalms: Those of the Desert

Something of the psalmist's perspective came to me while I was flying over the Sahara Desert. The desert is not flat and sandy brown. I saw high hills, long plateaus, deep caverns, and oases with thin traces of camel trails where the nomadic Tuareg drove their herds toward water. In the afternoon, the colors became soft browns under a hazy blue sky. Even later in the day, flying over the desert was like flying over a coral reef with deep green mineral deposits and organic shapes; in the early evening, the shades were a deep copper color with blue and purple shadows. Soon the stars appeared—first the Southern Cross, then thousands of other stars. I could almost read by their light.

Joseph Gelineau's musical psalm settings were current then, and I listened to a tape of them as we flew over the Sahara. The music was gentle and undulating, almost Moorish or Andalusian in mood, capturing both the majesty and the intimacy of God. The tape drew numerous images from the desert: "My soul thirsts for God" (Ps. 42); "the sun to govern the day . . . moon and stars to govern the night, his love is everlasting" (Ps. 136). "Let earth praise Yahweh . . . wild animals and farm animals, snakes and birds" (Ps. 148).

The unknown psalm writers had neither airplanes nor tape recorders when they wrote. Their perspectives were those of persons who saw Yahweh's universe as both the recipient of divine blessing and the giver, returning praise through all its parts. A key to reversing the present disorder is not only in praising God but in properly understanding dominion as responsible partnership and in understanding stewardship as the moderate use of creation, requiring replenishment where possible, and copartnership with the rest of the universe. A seventeenth-century English writer described humanity as "the viceroy of the great God, . . . [God's] steward, bailiff or farmer of this goodly farm of the lower world. Only for this reason was [humanity] invested with power, authority, right, dominion, trust and care . . . to preserve the face of the earth in beauty, usefulness and fruitfulness."[10]

A recent Methodist discussion of humanity's role in relation to creation stated the following:

> Alone of all earthly beings we possess reason and a capacity for self-transcendence, and thus for worship and prayer. We are to be stewards of the world on God's behalf, custodians of its amazing richness, companions to its variety of creatures, its "priests." We are to represent the whole created order to God, and to represent God within the creation. . . .
>
> God demands of us a radical change of attitude, so that at last we recognize our collective responsibility to become its stewards, custodians, friends, servants, priests.[11]

The priestly model of humanity's response to the environmental crisis is more encompassing than the idea of stewardship or of humanity as shepherds of the universe or as tillers of the soil and keepers of the earth (Gen. 2:15), although each of these concepts has merit. The difficulty with the stewardship idea is that, while the biblical steward acts admirably, it is essentially a passive role, acting responsibly but not taking much initiative. The concept of the shepherd is useful, but neither stewards nor shepherds understand the issue in its totality, nor is either in a position to respond to it in its complexity. Here humanity's priestly role can be helpful. If we understand the priestly role as both interpreting the divine understanding of creation and leading the ethical and liturgical response to it, we are establishing a model of human behavior for dealing with the crisis of belief and action facing the world.

A Wesleyan hymn "Love Divine, All Loves Excelling" contains the words *Finish, then, thy new creation*, which express the concept of continual creation. Genesis illustrates creation at the beginning of history, and Revelation or the "new heavens and a new earth" of Isaiah (65:17) depicts creation at history's end.

Genesis to Revelation: The Tree of Life

A tree is central to the garden of Eden, and the tree of life is an important final image in the Book of Revelation. The books of Ezekiel and Daniel contain significant tree passages. In biblical and devotional literature, tree images have several common traits: trees represent stages on which a political drama is enacted, such as the Crucifixion or the political destruction of Israel, or they link God and nature through suffering and redemption. The biblical trees are homes, shelters, and sources of life for many inhabitants. Their loss is tragic for nature and humanity.

Ezekiel (sixth century B.C.) 17:22-24 contains a messianic allegory. God says, "I, too, shall take a slip from the lofty crown of the cedar, and set it in the soil; I shall pluck a tender shoot from the topmost branch, and plant it on a high and lofty mountain" (v. 22). The branch is the Messiah, the lofty mountain Mount Zion. The tree will "become a noble cedar. Birds of every kind will roost under it, perching in the shelter of its boughs" (v. 23). All will know God's role in this process:

> All the trees of the countryside will know
> > that it is I, the LORD,
> > who bring low the tall tree,
> > and raise the lowly tree high,
> > who shrivel up the green tree
> > and make the shrivelled tree put forth buds.
> I, the LORD, have spoken; I shall do it.
> > > —Ezekiel 17:24

Pantheism is nonexistent in this and other Bible passages about nature. God created everything, and all matter is interconnected.

The tree is the setting for such interaction, and all participants find life and growth through praise of the prime Creator. Egypt's pharaoh does not praise God but asserts his own self-sufficiency. He will be destroyed, as a tree is cut down:

> Its sweeping boughs fell on the mountains and in all the valleys, and its branches lay broken beside every water-channel on earth. All the peoples of the earth came out from under its shade and left it. On its fallen trunk the birds all settled, the wild creatures all sought shelter among its branches. Never again will the well-watered trees grow so high or push their crowns up through the foliage. Nor will the strongest of them, though well-watered, attain their full height; for all have been given over to death, to the world below, to share the fate of mortals and go down to the abyss.
>
> —Ezekiel 31:12-13

In Daniel, the tree appears in a dream of King Nebuchadnezzar. The tree grows tall. It has rich foliage and abundant fruit, but a "holy one" demands that the tree be cut down. When the king asks for an interpretation, Daniel tells him that Nebuchadnezzar is the tree. His prideful actions will cause his downfall, his being cut down. Modern times transform the meaning of these Old Testament tree passages. Destroyers of the great trees and surrounding countryside are not external enemies but individuals and powers within society. The call for repentance is equal for all sectors of society—individual, governmental, and corporate.

Isaiah: A Shoot from the Stump of Jesse

The tree grows and is felled; the land is laid waste because people forsake Yahweh. Finally, a forgiving and generous God allows the tree to grow again. The Bible applies this recurring image equally to people and to their care of nature. Isaiah writes, "Then a branch will grow from the stock of Jesse, and a shoot will spring from his roots" (11:1). Yahweh "will shatter the trees with a crash," and

Lebanon's " noble trees will fall" (10:33-34). A new tree will grow, which is a metaphor for the new Israel, a kingdom with wisdom, understanding, and justice. Isaiah writes,

> The wolf will live with the lamb,
>   and the leopard lie down with the kid;
> the calf and the young lion will feed together,
>   with a little child to tend them (11:6).

In this peaceable kingdom, wild animals, poisonous vipers, and people will live together:

> There will be neither hurt nor harm
>   in all my holy mountain;
> for the land will be filled with the
>   knowledge of the LORD
> as the waters cover the sea (11:9).

In Second Isaiah, God is creator of both life and the world. These two manifestations of Yahweh are constant throughout history:

> Who has measured the waters of the
>   sea in the hollow of his hand,
> . . . .
> Who has held all the soil of the earth
>   in a bushel,
> or weighed the mountains on a
>   balance? (40:12)

For Second Isaiah, nature and God are inseparable. The environmental passages are not set apart like national parks; they disclose God's presence in history. These passages have a tender, redemptive quality. They were written after the destruction of the Temple and the Jewish dispersion in the Babylonian captivity:

> Rain righteousness, you heavens,
>   let the skies above pour it down,

let the earth open for it
that salvation may flourish
with righteousness growing beside it.
I the LORD have created this (45:8).

Break forth together into shouts of joy,
    you ruins of Jerusalem;
    for the LORD has comforted his people,
    he has redeemed Jerusalem (52:9).

The Land

The physical world has a distinct meaning for the Hebrew people. It is a gift from God. Biblical faith was not an abstract belief but specific laws set in the context of a distinctive historical setting, characterized by events like the Exodus and the quest for the promised land. Later, the Hebrew people abandoned God and were carried into exile. Then the wider Israel, the Israel of God, becomes a theme in biblical writings.

The land was filled with streams, springs, wheat and barley, fig trees, and pomegranates; its soil contained iron and copper. (See Deut. 8:7-10.) Planting and harvest, gentle rain and sudden tempest, small creatures and the cosmic order—all are part of the world that God entrusted to Israel. The yearning for land was a distinctive issue both in biblical times and today. Prayers at planting and harvesting were a feature of both Judaism and other Middle Eastern religions. In our own time, reverence for the land is a force reflected in the soil conservation movement in the 1930s, and some of the earliest and most articulate statements about Christian ecology come from denominations close to the land, especially in the Midwest.

I REFLECTED ON OLD TESTAMENT PASSAGES ABOUT LAND. The reverence for land played a part in my showing my family the place where I grew up, Oil City, a small northwestern Pennsylvania town in an economically depressed region.

46

We drove to a high hill overlooking what had once been the family farm; in this farmhouse, where my great aunts once lived, I spent countless summers as a child. The wooden house had a wide porch, gas lights, and large flower and vegetable gardens. Secret paths led from the gardens to orchards and an old cider press. I knew the apple trees, the great black walnut tree that cast a powerful presence against the horizon. Near it were large blackberry bushes and families of killdeer.

No trace of any of these memories remained. The ancestral home had been torn down to build a brick, two-story nursing school, which later closed for lack of applicants. The garden path, the curved avenue into childhood's kingdom, was now a vacant parking lot. A large field that I believed was the magical entrance to Dante's darkened wood was now a rolling, gentle lawn for a brick church. The hill's crest was once a cow pasture where we played two or three consecutive baseball games with a lopsided ball covered with heavy black electrician's tape. The field was now the site of a sprawling new high school.

I walked along both ridges, seeking tangible clues to recall the landscape of childhood. An apartment complex covered a spring our family gave the city, for which the family received free water in perpetuity. I do not know why, in excavating the past, I would seek springs or deeply rooted oak and walnut trees, except that both are important. Springs draw water from the earth's depths; trees grow from the earth and reach toward the sky. Both focus the mind and spirit, framing the environment, setting parameters for the rest of nature as a stage on which I enacted part of my childhood's drama. When I asked my brother, a local artist, what sustained him from his childhood, he replied, "God and those orchards."

I tried to recreate for my own family what the land meant to me as a child: In winter I could follow animal tracks and make tunnels through the snow. In spring, wild flowers pushed up through the earth, orchards filled with the smell of plum and pear blossoms, and I planted gardens. Summer was the long season of growth, when I lay in the sun and raced under the spray from a garden hose. In autumn, my family and I harvested grapes before the first frost, and canned vegetables, tomatoes, and spiced pears for the long winter.

The seasons' changes reflected the subtle changes in the church year, which marked transitions in our lives and in nature. An autumnal melancholy set in with the shortened days; the return of spring after a long, harsh winter was a foretaste of the Resurrection.

The spacious fields were also a place of healing and not only for the medicinal barks and plants that we boiled into teas. It was an ampitheater where I could act out the problems of home and school; an ordered cluster of apple trees became a school, a sheltered clump of field grass under the canopy of a huge walnut tree became a living room. Certain mud was good for extracting bee stings. Herbs and plants had curative powers. It was an enchanted realm, a continual Sabbath, not unlike the garden containing the "tree of life, which yields twelve crops of fruit, one for each month of the year. The leaves of the tree are for the healing of the nations" (Rev. 22:2).

Sabbath Time

Creation-related passages in the Old Testament lead to the Sabbath, the climax of existence, a feast without end. The Sabbath prefigures the world to come. All God's activity comes together in a state of eternal stillness and restfulness. Nature's constant fruitfulness finds completion in the Sabbath peace. The Sabbath blesses, sanctifies, and reveals creation. Jürgen Moltmann writes, "This divine peace encompasses not merely the soul but the body too; not merely individuals but family and people; not only human beings but animals as well; not living things alone, but also, as the Creation story tells us, the whole creation of heaven and earth."

Moltmann adds, "The sabbath peace is also the beginning of that peace with nature which many people are seeking today, in the face of the growing destruction of the environment. But there will never be peace with nature without the experience and celebration of God's sabbath."[12]

The seventh day of creation, as depicted in Genesis 2:2, is the day of God's rest, the time of blessing when the work of the previous six days is completed. The longest of the Ten Commandments is, "Remember to keep the sabbath day holy" (Ex. 20:8) and its related verses (9-11). It also states, "you must not do any work, neither you, nor your son or your daughter, your slave or your slave-girl, your cattle, or the alien residing among you" (Ex. 20:10).

The Sabbath concept is linked to life in the biosphere. Creation discloses God's handiwork, but the Sabbath reveals God's self. Moltmann draws on ancient Jewish teaching when he states that time and eternity intersect in the Sabbath. When we sanctify the Sabbath, we sanctify creation as well.

The Bible testifies to both a weekly Sabbath and a Sabbath year. Every seventh year, the Israelites are to give the land a sabbatical rest, and its produce is available to all, including strangers and animals. (See Lev. 25:1-11.) From earliest times, the Hebrews linked religion and land management. The nomads' exodus led through the desert to a land of milk and honey. Land laws were detailed. Land belonged to God and was held in trust by humanity, to pass on to future generations.

A recent Presbyterian study, *Keeping and Healing the Creation*, calls for "a right relationship with all of God's creation." It says, "The forgiving redeemer frees us, not for withdrawal from this world and contemplation of another, and not for community with our own kind only, but for right relationships with all of God's creation. We are to be nurtured by the realm of nature to 'till' and 'keep' it properly, and to participate in healing its afflictions."[13]

Older understandings of covenant and dominion do not help us in responding to the ecological crisis, nor do isolated fragments from individual passages. We look increasingly to Job and the Psalms to see the fullness of the divine presence in the universe's workings. Likewise, in the ancient Hebrew idea of the Sabbath, we see a vision of an ecologically sound world. In this world, resources are used prudently, and the biosphere and its contents are both cherished and used wisely. To complete a biblical understanding of God's mandate for an environmental ethic for our time, we need to examine the New Testament's creation-related passages.

Notes

1. "A Discussion Document on Christian Faith Concerning the Environment," *Floods and Rainbows: A Study Guide on the Environment—for Those who Care about the Future* (Methodist Church Division of Social Responsibility: London, 1991).

2. *The Book of Common Prayer* (New York: Oxford University Press, 1979), 42.

3. Michael Peers, address given to the ECUSA General Convention, Phoenix, Arizona, Open Hearing on the Environment, Thursday, July 11, 1991, 3.

4. Aldo Leopold, *A Sand County Almanac* (New York: Oxford University Press, 1966), 129–30.

5. Sermon at National Cathedral, Washington, D.C., 16 June 1991.

6. Edith Brown Weiss, "In Fairness to Future Generations," *Environment*, Vol. 32, No. 3, April 1990, 8.

7. American Bar Association, Annual Meeting, Chicago, Illinois, 8 August 1990.

8. Paraphrased from *The Oxford Cycle of Prayer* (London: Oxford University Press, 1986) and "Coping with Climate Change," Intergovernmental Panel on Climate Change (Geneva, World Meteorological Organization, August 1990), 2–3.

9. Hugh Montefiore, ed., *Man and Nature* (London: Collins, 1975), 88.

10. Matthew Hale, *The Primitive Organization of Mankind* (London, 1677), 370, quoted in Ian Bradley's *God Is Green* (London: Darton, Longman, and Todd, 1990), 91.

11. *Floods and Rainbows.*

12. Jürgen Moltmann, *God in Creation: A New Theology of Creation and the Spirit of God* (San Francisco: Harper & Row, 1985), 277.

13. *Keeping and Healing the Creation* (Louisville: Committee on Social Witness Policy, Presbyterian Church, USA, 1989), 50.

Two

The New Testament

W HEN I WAS A CHILD IN WESTERN PENNSYLVANIA, *each*
spring my great-aunts would send me to Seep's
hardware store to buy seed for our farm. The
hardware store, a rickety wooden building on Oil City's main
street, was the entrance to a mysterious kingdom. The
rectangular, two-story structure, built during the oil boom,
was lighted poorly and overcrowded. Shining new tin buckets
hung from nails, lengths of rope dangled from pegs, hoes and
rakes of all sizes were stacked in corners. Along the western
wall was a row of deep, dark wooden seed bins. The dividing
boards were thick, smeared a Rembrandtesque brown from
decades of hands scooping out onions, beans, peas, wheat,
and grasses. Each seed had a distinct size and color. There
were smooth, circular lima beans with shiny veneer like
Chinese jade, fragrant dill seeds, and dry seed corn that
rattled as it fell quickly through fingers.

The annual seed purchase followed lengthy winter
discussions. The two great-aunts and Uncle Henry spent
evenings at the dining room table, illuminated by a gas light,
reviewing the previous year's experience with flowers and
vegetables, weighing the merit of Mr. Seep's seeds against the

claims in Burpee's illustrated catalog. When the locally purchased order was bundled into small brown paper sacks, the seeds pushing against the paper, I tucked them into a wicker basket and headed up the hill toward home.

The house stirred at winter's end. The fields must be plowed, which meant arranging things with a busy farmer who had no phone, who walked behind his horse and metal plow, knifing the brown earth open in straight lines. Worms were unearthed, stones halved, and occasional Indian arrowheads uncovered. Like liturgists distributing consecrated bread, we dropped handfuls of corn seed into the earth, or the more evenly spaced beans into larger holes. The smell of rich brown earth lasted for hours. The land was alive with the buzz of insects and the chirping of birds.

"THE SOIL IS THE GREAT CONNECTOR OF OUR LIVES, the source and destination of all," Wendell Berry writes. "It is healer and restorer and resurrector, by which disease passes into health, age into youth, death into life. . . . Given only the health of the soil, nothing that dies is dead for very long. Within this powerful economy, it seems that death occurs only for the good of life."[1]

The connection between Easter and ecology is a useful point of departure to examine New Testament issues about Christ and creation. We are only beginning to understand the Paschal Mystery and its relationship to nature. But we discover clues to its depth in several events of the Easter season, including the Harrowing of Hell, Christ's descent to the place of the dead. According to Christian tradition, the interval between Christ's death and resurrection included a visit by Christ to the place where the spirits of the just from the time of Eve and Adam awaited liberation. Icons of the event depict the risen Christ pulling Adam and Eve up by their arms. Death's shrouds are parted, metal bands are snapped in two, and the protoancestors' arms are almost dislocated by the quick pull skyward.

Christ's descent into the earth has meaning for both humans and nature. "No less than the faithful of religion is the good farmer mindful of the persistence of life through death, the passage of energy through changing forms," Berry writes.[2] The redemptive power of Easter manifests both energy and mystery; the dark earth that receives the body of Christ is simultaneously the nurturing womb holding life's seed.

The Christian doctrine of the Resurrection includes both humans and nature. Nature participates in both the desolation of Christ's crucifixion and the joyful resurrection in an Easter garden. Jesus is "lying in the grave, like a corn of wheat buried under the clods for a time," a Puritan divine, Gerrard Winstanley writes, adding, "The body of Christ is where the Father is, in the earth, purifying the earth; and his Spirit is entered into the whole creation, which is the heavenly glory where the Father dwells."[3] An affinity exists between Christ and the earth. Earth is the vessel that receives the crucified savior's body; the discovery of Christ's resurrection occurs in an Easter garden. An Easter hymn expresses this idea:

> Now the green blade riseth, from the buried grain,
> Wheat that in the dark earth many days has lain;
> Love lives again, that with the dead has been:
> Love is come again, like wheat that springeth green.
>
> In the grave they laid him, Love who had been slain,
> Thinking that he never would wake again,
> Laid in the earth like grain that sleeps unseen:
> Love is come again, like wheat that springeth green.
>
> Forth he came at Easter, like the risen grain,
> Jesus who for three days in the grave had lain,
> Quick from the dead my risen Lord is seen:
> Love is come again, like wheat that springeth green.[4]

Numerous Easter garden images depict the relationship between Christ and creation. E. B. White describes the final days of his wife, an avid gardener. She sat in a director's chair, in overly large clothing, presiding at the autumn interment of bulbs in their Maine garden. He spoke of seeing her figure in the garden, small and hunched-over. She sat there, not giving thought to her own imminent death. Under the dark skies of dying October, she sat in her garden with her detailed chart and calmly plotted the resurrection.

The most striking feature about the New Testament's ecologically related passages is their compactness and focus on Christ's life and teachings. The New Testament writers develop positions clearly but not extensively. New Testament writers assume familiarity with older biblical narratives and theology. The Old Testament's considerable nature poetry is absent, which does not mean less concern about the relationship between God and nature, only that it is transformed.

The Incarnation

The Easter gospels fully express the New Testament's unity between Christ and creation, but other New Testament events such as the Incarnation, Crucifixion, and Transfiguration also bear witness to this unity. The prologue to the Gospel of John, which parallels creation accounts in Genesis 1, elaborates on the Incarnation. In John's Gospel, divinity and nature unite in a single life, Jesus the Christ, the Creator's human embodiment. The Old Testament creation passages telescope into a single life. Nature and God converge; the primal Word, source of light and life, becomes flesh and makes its home among us, full of grace and truth. The Incarnation, likewise, brings the divine presence to all nature and all humanity, past and present; it is a cosmic event, reaffirming the sanctity of all creation and God's loving presence in both the crevices of existence and the biosphere.

For the French scientist-cleric, Pierre Teilhard de Chardin, God is physically active in the universe in the movement of atoms and in the labyrinths of creative human thought. In recent religious writings, he depicts the Incarnation in this way: "Everything that is good in the Universe . . . is gathered up by the Incarnate Word."

Sometimes we understand religious ideas more easily when we hear them expressed in folk idiom. "The Cherry Tree Carol" describes the Incarnation poetically as the tree blooms out of season and bows low at the Christ child's birth. Art of the Christmas season depicts Jesus lying on a bed of straw, kept warm by the breath of surrounding field animals. The birth in the stable becomes a redemptive act for humanity and nature.

Orthodoxy has long held a comparable vision of the Incarnation. A twentieth-century Orthodox theologian, Paul Evdokimov, wrote the following:

> The destiny of the element of water is to participate in the mystery of the Epiphany; the destiny of the earth is to receive the body of the Lord for the repose of the Great Saturday; and the destiny of stone is to end as the "sealed tomb" and as the stone rolled away before the myrrh-bearing women. Olive oil and water find their fulfilment as conductors of grace to regenerated [humanity]; the wheat and the vine culminate in the Eucharistic cup. Everything refers to the Incarnation, and everything leads to the Lord.[5]

Jesus' Teaching Ministry and Nature

During his life, Jesus often used images of the natural world—animals, plants, and changes of the seasons. The Galilean countryside through which he traveled was the setting for numerous parables. Like other Jews, Jesus knew the teachings of the Hebrew scriptures about God and creation. Jesus described yeast, wheat, vines and vineyards, the salt of the earth, and the light of the world. He told followers, "Look at the birds in the sky . . . and how the lilies grow in the fields," and reminded them that "Solomon in all his splendor was not attired like one of them" (Matt. 6:26, 28, 29).

The good tree yields sound fruit, the sower casts seed onto good soil. The kingdom of heaven is like yeast mixed with flour until it is leavened or like a mustard seed, a small seed that grows into a plant large enough for birds to roost in its branches. Jesus urges followers to learn from the common fig tree. (See Matt. 24:32-34.) The changes in its leaves reflect seasonal changes, and "in the same way, when you see all these things, you may know that the end is near, at the very door" (Matt. 24:33). When his followers ate ears of corn plucked on the sabbath, Jesus responded to the heckling Pharisees' objections with these words: "The Son of Man is lord of the sabbath" (Matt. 12:8).

Jesus spoke of foxes having their holes and birds their roosts, but he had nowhere to lay his head. Jesus frequently used the image of himself as a shepherd; his followers were like sheep. He compared the end of the age to a harvest. Once, when Jesus and his closest followers were in a boat on a lake, a storm arose. Jesus calmed the storm; his followers exclaimed, "What sort of man is this? Even the wind and the sea obey him" (Matt. 8:27). Jesus was aware of the natural world around him and of its link to the God of all creation. An English Methodist document states, "Jesus in his ministry delighted in the world, in nature, and taught us to see in it the signs of God's providential care. In him the rule of God's kingdom was made plain, but not like earthly rule. He rode upon an ass, and we see in the sacrificial lamb the sign of his own kingly self-offering. He bore in himself the sin and agony and tragedy of our human condition. He represented all creation. "[6]

The Transfiguration

While Western Christians see the unity of God and creation in the Incarnation, Eastern Christians find the unity of God and nature in New Testament times particularly evident in the Transfiguration. Both the Incarnation and the Transfiguration are central events in Orthodox belief; both suggest the infusion of God's presence in all life.

Orthodox believers express this approach to religion in doctrine as well as in church architecture. Traditional Orthodox churches are built with careful attention to their natural sur-roundings. They have no stained glass windows with biblical messages, but often they have recessed light wells that allow light to enter the building in a soft, diffuse, mystical way. The warm glow creates a transforming ethos where each element retains its individuality yet contributes to the transformed whole.

Mark 9:2-18 and Luke 9:28-36 describe the Transfiguration. Shortly before his final entry into Jerusalem, Jesus and some disciples climb a high mountain, possibly Mount Tabor, near Jerusalem. Jesus is transfigured: "His clothes became dazzling white, with a whiteness no bleacher on earth could equal" (Mark 9:3). Two personalities from the Old Testament, Moses, first of the prophets, and Elijah, an important later prophet, join Jesus and his followers. The voice from the cloud indicates the presence of God: "This is my beloved Son; listen to him" (Mark 9:7).

The Orthodox church commemorates the Transfiguration as a separate feast day, August 6; Western churches increasingly observe it. The celebration of the Transfiguration calls the world to a new level of awareness. It is a transforming mountaintop experience that places all creation in a new light, just as John's Gospel suffuses the Incarnation with glory. Icons picture the transfigured Christ. The biblical figures, the mountain, animals, and vegetation reflect the radiance of Christ's glory. Transfigured by Christ, a strong light fills creation. Light and warmth are ancient symbols of creation and the victory over primal elements. The sun is the symbol of energy. The Transfiguration unites all creation with its Creator.

One little-known aspect of the Transfiguration as celebrated in the Orthodox churches is the distribution of grapes at the liturgy's end. This distribution suggests a harvest festival, perhaps related to the shortened growing season in some Slavic countries. The prayer says, "Bless, O Lord this new fruit of the vine, which Thou hast been pleased to bring to full ripeness through temperate seasons, showers of rain, and calm weather."[7]

The Crucifixion

Christ's suffering on Good Friday is for humanity and for nature as well; through his suffering, creation gains new life. The Atonement means Christ's being at one with the distressed. A merciful God is also with wild creatures and suffering animals—those bearing pain in laboratories, and those crowded in commercial food pens without rest or exercise. A gentle savior is with dolphins caught in giant commercial tuna nets, with fur-bearing creatures destroyed for their pelts, and with wolves chased across the tundra by hunters firing automatic rifles from airplanes and snowmobiles. A Methodist commentary states that "as God's Son and servant, the whole misery of the universe was expressed in his death. Jesus as the 'light of the universe' was one through whom God chose to reconcile the universe to [God's] self. It was as if all creation tasted the depths of death in Christ's dying."[8]

In Matthew's account, the Crucifixion disrupts nature. Darkness covers the land during the three hours Christ suffers on the cross. At the moment of Christ's death, an earthquake occurs; the Temple's curtain tears in two, rocks split, and graves open. (See Matt. 27:45, 51-55.) Mark's account (15:33-39) is similar. Luke says "the sun's light failed" (23:45). Nature protests the murder of God with such voice allowed it. Biblical commentators increasingly view the Old and New Testaments' numerous theophanies, not as dramatic embellishments of verbal messages, but as divine manifestations that link God, nature, and humanity.

Christ was crucified on a tree and that central event in his life resulted in a rich outpouring of tree-related images. The tree bears the dying body of the holy one; it is the kindly, silent recipient of the suffering God. In religious writings, some such trees later sprout flowers. Appalachian children are taught that the dark stains on dogwood blossoms come from drops of Christ's blood spilt as the tree witnessed the Crucifixion.

Dame Julian of Norwich links Christ's crucifixion and nature's suffering: "For when He was in pain, we were in pain. And all creatures that might suffer pain, suffered with Him: that is to say, all creatures that God hath made to our service."[9]

Darkness covering the earth on Good Friday and disturbances of nature demonstrate for Moltmann the earth's solidarity with Christ's suffering: "In the light of creation, the cross of Christ means the true consolation of the universe. Because from the very beginning the Creator is prepared to suffer in this way for [God's] creation, [the] creation endures to eternity. The cross is the mystery of creation and the promise of its future."[10]

The symbol of the Lamb of God links the suffering God and nature's desolation. The Lamb's sacrifice helps usher in the kingdom of God, where all creation finds welcome. "Worthy is the Lamb who was slain, to receive power and wealth, wisdom and might, honour and glory and praise" (Rev. 5:12). The lamb, vulnerable and silent, was the traditional victim of blood sacrifices and an image of Christ on the cross. In the Fourth Servant passage in Second Isaiah the disfigured Servant remains silent "like a sheep led to the slaughter" (53:7). The analogy with the destruction of nature is evident.

All humanity is of the earth and, after a span of years, returns to the earth. "Remember that you are dust, and to dust you shall return," the Ash Wednesday liturgy states. The Creator gives each living thing, at its birth, a loan of chemical elements, which return to earth at death.

In *Deserts on the March*, the naturalist Paul Sears wrote, "No plant or animal . . . can establish permanent right of possession. Left to herself, nature manages these loans and redemptions in not unkindly fashion. She maintains a balance which will permit the briefest time to elapse between burial and renewal. The turnover of material for new generations to use is steady and regular. Wind and water, those twin sextons, do their work as gently as may be."[11]

The Universe in Travail

Paul's letters provide the New Testament's most complete description of Christ's link to creation, including the knowledge that both humans and nature await redemption through Christ. Nature, like humanity, is a victim of transience and death. This estrangement does not come from any sinful act on nature's part. Humans cause estrangement from God, which reflects humanity's self-willed separation from its Creator. Paul's writings depict the natural world with autumnal melancholy and a yearning for release from bondage, which it suffers but did not cause. Two passages express this idea: from Romans, "The whole created universe in all its parts groans as if in the pangs of childbirth. What is more, we . . . are groaning inwardly while we look forward eagerly to our adoption, our liberation from mortality" (8:22-23).

Redemption comes through the risen Christ. In Philippians: "Therefore God raised him to the heights and bestowed on him the name above all names, that at the name of Jesus every knee should bow—in heaven, on earth, and in the depths—and every tongue acclaim, 'Jesus Christ is Lord,' to the glory of God the Father" (2:9-11).

Paul argues that humanity's liberation through Christ is for the universe and its elements; the Fall affects all creation. As the Psalms reveal an orderly universe in the midst of discordant forces, Paul views creation as exposed to birthpangs, futility, and hope. In both cases, struggle and chaos exist. Human beings wreak devastation but so do storms and natural disasters. While insurance policies call these "acts of God," they are anything but that. God, having created the world, does not manipulate its daily operations. Humanity received the norms of conduct. History records humanity's observance and violation of these rules and their consequences in our time; the earth is the stage for this struggle.

Paul, in Colossians, describes a universe closely linked to God; to wound it is to strike out at its creator.

> He [Christ] is the image of the invisible God; his is the primacy over all creation. In him everything in heaven and on earth was created, not only things visible but also the invisible. . . . He exists before all things, and all things are held together in him. . . . For in him God in all his fullness chose to dwell, and through him to reconcile all things to himself, making peace through the shedding of his blood on the cross—all things, whether on earth or in heaven (1:15-16, 17, 19-20).

Later Paul equates baptism with the Crucifixion and the Resurrection. "For you were buried with him in baptism, and in that baptism you were also raised to life with him through your faith in the active power of God, who raised him from the dead" (Col.

2:12). In this process Paul asks, "Did you not die with Christ and pass beyond reach of the elemental spirits of the universe?" (2:20) Here the cosmic hope of all estranged creation, as described in Romans 8, finds fulfillment.

The great events of Holy Week mean that through Christ "the universe itself is to be freed from the shackles of mortality and is to enter upon the glorious liberty of the children of God" (Rom. 8:21). All creation has unity and interaction among its parts, and if it was estranged from the Fall, it participates in the great redemptive act of the Crucifixion and the Resurrection. Now the morning stars sing in chorus and the children of God all shout for joy, to paraphrase Job 38:7. The Apostle Paul's writings link God with creation from within, not outside the universe. God is the earth's creator, sustainer, and redeemer. God is present in the universe, displaying patience, vulnerability, and solidarity with earth's weak and threatened creatures.

The idea of God's activity in creation is analogous to the perspective of a contemporary physicist who studies structures of inert, solid matter and, under intense magnification, finds them full of motion and energy. Paul Tillich concludes,

> The world process means something for God. [God] is not a separated, self-sufficent entity. . . . Rather, the eternal act of creation is driven by a love which finds fulfillment only through the other one who has the freedom to reject and accept love. God, so to speak, drives toward the actualization and essentialization of everything that has being. For the eternal dimension of what happens in the universe it is the Divine life itself. It is the content of divine blessedness.[12]

For Claus Westermann, the fact that the Bible begins with creation—heaven and earth, the sun, moon and stars, growing things, birds, fish, and animals—is indicative that God has concern for all of these creatures, not only humans. A God who is *only* the God of humankind is not the God of the Bible.

The austere New England Calvinist Jonathan Edwards recognized this idea. Edwards employed an image of love's holding the universe together, working like a gravitational force in the physical world. Edwards finds a place among nature and spirituality writers. "The whole material world is preserved by gravity or attraction, or the mutual tendency of all bodies to each other. One part of the universe is hereby made beneficial to another; the beauty, harmony and order, regular progress, life and motion, and in short all the well-being of the whole frame depends on it. This is a type of love or charity in the spiritual world."[13]

Christ's life is linked with all creation. When the cosmic word became flesh and entered history at the Incarnation, it came as a nurturing, protecting, judging, and sustaining force. We see this message in countless nativity scenes and Christmas carols. Through the Crucifixion and the Atonement, Christ emptied himself in love. As God's creatures, humans can engage in loving relationships with all creation. This relationship is the historic idea of *imago dei*, of creation in God's image. This relationship asks humans to widen their love of God and neighbor to include inarticulate creation and the extra-human world. A Methodist writer states,

> In Jesus we see God's nature most fully expressed, and find God most significantly and decisively at work. . . . If much traditional piety has seen him as the savior of all human beings, we in our time, aware of the creation as an independent whole, see him as the saviour of the complete cosmos. In the resurrection, we see God pointing forward to the glory of the final end of all things. Jesus represents creation fulfilled, redeemed, put right. A new covenant has come about.[14]

Creation, Baptism, and Eucharist

As Old Testament creation theology merges in the Sabbath idea, so the New Testament unites baptism and the Eucharist as the continual link between God and creation. Here, again, we find initiation into the created order followed by the messianic banquet, the feast without end. God invites God's children to the celestial gathering and seeks to give them an earthly paradise as well, both filled with plentiful foods, beautiful fragrances, and plants for healing. In the New Testament, we move beyond traditional understandings of covenant and dominion to a wider, more complex union between God and creation.

In the New Testament, Christ provides the unity between Creator and creation. In baptism and the offering of bread and wine, Christ uses products of the earth to feed and maintain God's children. This expanded idea of creation represents a historic strain in Christian belief, albeit one often ignored until recent times. Paul Tillich writes, "Bread and wine, water and light, and all the great elements of nature become the bearers of spiritual meaning and saving power. Natural and spiritual powers are united—reunited—in the sacrament."[15]

In each baptism and Eucharist, Christians take the concrete gifts of water, bread, and wine from God's universe, fashion them with human hands, and prayerfully return them as gifts to a loving creator. We include the universe in the sacramental action of receiving gifts from God and returning thanks for them. Otherwise, our action is incomplete. Fundamental acts of human praise should include creation and its contents, from the biosphere in its beauty and wonder to the most minute, silent creatures.

Several baptismal prayers express this idea. The Thanksgiving Over the Water in the United Methodist Baptismal Covenant I is a concise statement of biblical creation theology:

> Eternal Father:
> When nothing existed but chaos,
>   you swept across the dark waters
>   and brought forth light.
> In the days of Noah
>   you saved those on the ark through water.
> After the flood you set in the clouds a rainbow.
> . . . .
> When you saw your people as slaves in Egypt,

you led them to freedom through the sea.
Their children you brought through the Jordan
   to the land which you promised.
. . . .
In the fullness of time you sent Jesus,
   nurtured in the water of a womb.
He was baptized by John and anointed by your Spirit.
He called his disciples
      to share in the baptism of his death and
      resurrection
   and to make disciples of all nations.
. . . .
Pour out your Holy Spirit,
to bless this gift of water and *those* who *receive* it,
to wash away *their* sin
   and clothe *them* in righteousness
   throughout *their lives*,
that, dying and being raised with Christ,
they may share in his final victory.[16]

The Episcopal *Book of Common Prayer*'s Thanksgiving Over the Water at baptism contains a similar concept: "We thank you, Almighty God, for the gift of water. Over it the Holy Spirit moved in the beginning of creation. Through it you led the children of Israel out of their bondage in Egypt into the land of promise. In it your Son Jesus received the baptism of John and was anointed by the Holy Spirit as the Messiah, the Christ, to lead us, through his death and resurrection, from the bondage of sin into everlasting life."[17]

Like baptism, the Eucharist is a central expression of the sacramental relationship between creation and God, transformed by the Holy Spirit to be both God's and the means of human praise.

Among recent writers, the creation-creator-humanity link is most explicit in the writings of the Jesuit priest-poet-scientist Pierre Teilhard de Chardin. During an extended period in World War I, and again on an expedition in China's Gobi Desert in 1923, he was unable to offer mass. During that time, he composed a set of eucharistic prayers, which he reworked and never published in final form. These prayers are known as "The Mass on the World."

The prayers employ parallel constructs of growth and diminishment, expansion and contraction. For example, the offertory asks God to receive the all-encompassing host that God's whole creation offers God this day. Then he asks God to receive the all-encompassing wine that God's whole creation offers God this day. For Teilhard, the bread expands to include the universe and its contents in germination; the wine, squeezed from grapes, is part of life that is extracted, consumed, and diminished. At the communion, participants state that as they stretch their hands toward the bread, they surrender themselves to the forces that dilate the universe; while the earth itself will enable them to contemplate the face of God.

In the wine, they pour the bitterness of all separations, all limitations, and all fallings away. Creation and Christ unite in the postcommunion prayer. The prayer acknowledges Christ as the divine influence and center where all meet. It is to Christ that our whole being cries out its desire that is as vast as the universe: "In truth you are our Lord and our God."

Notes

1. Quoted in Carolyn Tanner Irish, ed., *Love Thy Neighbor*, Environment Committee of the Peace Commission, Diocese of Washington, D.C., 1991, 36.

2. Ibid.

3. Quoted in Ian Bradley, *God Is Green* (London: Darton, Longman & Todd, 1990), 80.

4. Verified from *The United Methodist Hymnal* (Nashville, TN: The United Methodist Publishing House, 1989), 311.

5. Paul Evdokimov, "Nature," *Scottish Journal of Theology*, Vol. 18, No. 1, March 1965, 15.

6. "A Discussion Document on Christian Faith Concerning the Environment," *Floods and Rainbows: A Study Guide on the Environment—for Those who Care about the Future* (Methodist Church Division of Social Responsibility: London, 1991).

7. Mother Mary and Kallistos Ware, *The Festal Menaion* (London: Faber and Faber, 1969), 502.

8. *Floods and Rainbows*.

9. Grace Warrack, ed., *Revelations of Divine Love* recorded by Julian, Anchoress at Norwich (London: Methuen, 1901), 40–41.

10. Jürgen Moltmann, *God in Creation* (San Francisco: Harper Collins Paperback, 1991), 91.

11. Paul Bigelow Sears, *Deserts on the March* (Norman: University of Oklahoma Press, 1940), 1. Quoted in Daniel B. Botkin, *Discordant Harmonies* (New York: Oxford University Press, 1990).

12. Paul Tillich, *Systematic Theology*, Vol. III (Chicago: The University of Chicago Press, 1967), 422.

13. Quoted in George S. Hendry, *Theology of Nature* (Philadelphia: The Westminster Press, 1980), 63–64.

14. *Floods and Rainbows*.

15. Paul Tillich, *The Shaking of the Foundations* (New York: Charles Scribner's Sons, 1948), 86.

16. *The United Methodist Hymnal* (Nashville, TN: The United Methodist Publishing House, 1989), 36.

17. *The Book of Common Prayer* (New York: Oxford University Press, 1990), 306.

Part II

*Ecology
and the
Christian
Church*

Three

The Early Church

THE SEPARATION BETWEEN GOD AND CREATION that influences much modern writing did not exist in the early church—Eastern, Western, or Celtic. Early Christian writers merit careful reading, not only for the freshness of their writing, but because much of what the modern church is wrestling with as creation and ecology issues was already spoken to by these amazing figures.

Irenaeus of Lyons

Irenaeus of Lyons, for example, a second century Asia Minor prelate, was a voice for an inclusive doctrine of creation. Like many of his contemporaries, Irenaeus believed humanity was living in the Sixth Day, awaiting the imminent Second Coming.

Irenaeus saw God as the prime creator. The bridge between Creator and created universe was the Incarnation, when the word became flesh in specific historical circumstances. The fulfillment of history would come in the Seventh Day, the sabbath of God, toward which it moved.

Irenaeus explained the movement of humanity and history toward the end of the age as a pilgrimage toward the good land, a place of fecundity, fertility, and plenty; a land that contained everything God's pilgrim people required or desired. He employed a trinitarian formula of the Father as creator-planner, the Son as the action agent, and the Spirit as nurturer who increased the activity of the other two.

A subtle balance exists in Irenaeus's thought among God, humanity, and nature. A modern Lutheran commentator has written of Irenaeus:

> God is one who contains all things, works richly in them, gives them their individual places within the whole, and thus bestows harmony on all things. . . . The divine governance moreover, has a certain nurturant, embracing character in Irenaeus's view; God surely does not dominate the earth as some alien, despotic other. Accordingly, human dominion over nature is a muted, not to say scarcely visible, theme for Irenaeus. The accent is . . . on *communion*—eating in the midst of the overflowing blessings that God gives in nature.[1]

Irenaeus himself described the deep tie between Creator and created: "And as we are [God's] members, we are also nourished by means of the creation (and [God] grants the creation to us, for [God] causes the sun to rise, and sends rain when [God] wills). [God] has acknowledged the cup (which is part of [the] creation) as [God's] own blood, from which [God] renews our blood; and the bread (also part of the creation) [the Creator] has established as [God's] own body, from which [God] gives increase to our bodies."[2]

Irenaeus's thought comes to us in fragments. His creation theology is not highly developed; for Irenaeus, like his contemporaries in the Mediterranean basin churches, lived in a world where the divorce between nature and God was yet to occur. Irenaeus appeared to cherish the biosphere and its contents as a gift from God. His writing was not unlike that of such Asia Minor theologians as Isaac of Syria or John of Damascus.

Isaac of Syria

Like the Christian writers of the first six centuries who see God's creative presence in the natural order, early Orthodox spirituality is rich in creation-and-nature imagery. Orthodox spirituality is diffuse, mystical, overlapping, circular, and anything but logical and rational. Orthodoxy offers a rich view of the possibilities of the redemption of all creation that any religious discussion about the environment sorely needs.

In one prayer by Isaac of Syria, a seventh century A.D. bishop in what is now Iraq, Isaac describes a heart that is on fire for all creation—for humanity, birds, animals. The compassionate heart of God cannot bear the slightest suffering of anything in creation. In Isaac's understanding, God prays even for the irrational animals.

When John Chrysostom describes creation, he uses language not unlike that found in Genesis and Job:

> Look at the sky, how beautiful it is, and how vast, all crowned with a blazing diadem of stars! . . .
>
> Look at the great mass of the mountains, and all the innumerable people who dwell on earth, and the planets, all so rich and wonderfully varied, and the town and the vast buildings and the wild animals, and all these the earth supports easily on her back. And yet with all its vastness, it was fashioned by God as though it were nothing. . . . Think of all the peoples who inhabit the earth: Syrians, Cilicians, Cappadocians, Bithynians, those who live on the shores of the Black Sea, in Thrace, in Macedonia, in all Greece and the islands and in Italy, and beyond the places well-known to us, think of the islands of Britain, Sarmatia, India, and the inhabitants of Persia, and then of all the innumerable other peoples and races, and all these are as a "drop of water falling from a bowl." And what small atom of this drop of water thinks [it] can know God?[3]

Orthodox thought clearly draws the line between pantheism (finding gods in nature) and incarnational spirituality (finding God's presence in all creation). Saint John of Damascus, an eighth century A.D. writer, expresses this distinction:

> I do not worship matter. I worship the Creator of matter who became matter for my sake, who willed to take [God's] abode in matter; who worked out my salvation through matter. Never will I cease honoring the matter which wrought my salvation! I honor it, but not as God. . . . Because of this I salute all remaining matter with reverence, because God has filled it with [God's] grace and power. Through it my salvation has come to me.[4]

The contemporary Orthodox theologian Paul Evdokimov comprehensively portrays the relationship between nature and Christ:

> Christ walked this earth: He admired its flowers, and in His parables He spoke of the things of this world as figures of the heavens; He was baptized in the waters of the Jordan, He spent three days in the bosom of the earth; there is nothing in this world which has remained a stranger to His humanity and has not received the imprint of the Holy Spirit. And that is why the Church in turn blesses and sanctifies all creation: greenery and flowers fill the churches on the day of Pentecost; the Feast of the Epiphany is accompanied by "the great sanctification of the waters and of all the matter of the cosmos"; in the evening office on the eve of great feasts, the church blesses the grains of wheat, the oil, the bread and the wine—the representative species of nature and its fecundity; on the day of the Elevation of the Cross, the Church blesses the four corners of the world and so places the whole plane of nature in obeisance under the saving sign of the invincible Cross.[5]

The Celtic Tradition

Modern Christians, seeking historical sources of creation spirituality, will find riches in the Celtic Church, which, had it survived, might have prevented the split between God and nature that widened through the centuries. Many issues bearing on a religious understanding of the ecological crisis have deep roots in Celtic religious thought. In addition to Celtic authors, numerous English-speaking writers have evoked the presence of such a world of wonder and mystery, with God at the center as creator of all matter, including the biosphere and its contents. The Holy Spirit's activity affirms God's continual presence in creation. A goal of Christian society is to work for the sanctification of all life, including life in the biosphere.

Celtic prayers, like those collected by Alexander Carmichael (1832–1912), who moved about the Outer Hebrides for over sixty years, recording prayers and hymns of the isolated communities off Scotland's northwest coast, give evidence to the tie between God and nature. The goal of Celtic prayer was the sanctification of all life. They included prayers for the sun and moon, saints and angels, day and night, planting and harvest, birth and death, and for such daily acts as milking cows and covering the fire.

Many of the prayers include animals, like this Reaping Blessing:

> Encompass each goat, sheep and lamb,
> Each cow and horse, and store,
> Surround Thou the flocks and herds,
> And tend them to a kindly fold.[6]

The prayers incorporate fishing, ocean, and herding blessings, as well as prayers for the protection of cattle:

> Closed be every pit to you,
> Smoothed be every knoll to you,
> Cosy every exposure to you.
> Beside the cold mountains,
>   Beside the cold mountains.[7]

Even shorter prayers and blessings draw on the natural order:

> Wisdom of serpent be thine,
> Wisdom of raven be thine,
>   Wisdom of valiant eagle.
>
> Voice of swan be thine,
> Voice of honey be thine,
>   Voice of the son of the stars.
>
> Bounty of sea be thine,
> Bounty of land be thine,
>   Bounty of the Father of heaven.[8]

Celtic prayer, like Celtic art, wove commonplace and cosmic together; it encircled and encompassed the person praying with the cosmos and its creator.

Among sacred places, Christians revere no setting more than the small island off Scotland, where Saint Columba and his monks settled in A.D. 563. Describing the Western Highlands, A. M. Allchin wrote,

> Perhaps nowhere else in Christendom is there such a moving expression of the sense of the all-pervasive presence of God with us, throughout the day and in every circumstance: a sense that even in the smallest details of life on earth as well as heaven is full of God's glory.[9]

The Way of Praise

The Advent season raises the question humanity faces, Christmas answers it; we reexperience it on Good Friday, and Easter affirms it. The journey is from darkness to light, from chaos to creation. At the same time humanity's inclination is to play God, to sin; the visible evidence of that sin is pollution and destruction of Planet Earth and its biosphere.

What does the future hold? We are not sure. If the data is deeply troubling, the landscape remains ultimately hopeful. But we have no assurance of a hero on a white horse who will arrive at the last moment to save the world. How does Christianity speak to this issue? We need to accept a joyous, loving Creator, the giver of gifts beyond price. Our love must be equally self-giving and grace-filled, first in return to God, then toward the entire creation. We express this love in numerous ways, from giving thanks to God for the beauty of creation to working for the environmental agenda that is a part of global peace and justice initiatives.

Action gains new life if informed by praise. And if praise is so encompassing as to include other humans, plants and animals, the earth and biosphere, we will recognize what the biblical writers knew all along: Praise of God is praise of God's creation; God's handiwork manifests the divine joy. Humanity's role is both returning thanks to God and creating conditions that allow others to give thanks in their time. God and creation call us to a new, transfigured vision of the cosmic Christ's leadership; to follow not as a species apart, but as those given responsible, accountable dominion as inheritors of God's bounty.

Photographs of Planet Earth taken from the moon changed the centuries-old cosmic vision of poets, geographers, and planetary scientists forever. The colored globe, like the rose window of a Gothic cathedral, reflects divine gifts and human creativity and reduces a cosmic perspective to an understandable image. As the cathedral's preservation in modern times is an enduring challenge, so is the preservation of Planet Earth.

Notes

1. H. Paul Santmire, *The Travail of Nature: The Ambiguous Ecological Promise of Christian Theology* (Philadelphia: Fortress Press, 1985), 43–44.

2. Irenaeus, *Against the Heresies*, 5.2.2., quoted in H. Paul Santmire, *The Travail of Nature: The Ambiguous Ecological Promise of Christian Theology* (Philadelphia: Fortress Press, 1985), 41–42.

3. John Chrysostom, *De Incomprehensibili*, II, 6, in Robert Payne, *The Holy Fire* (New York: Harper & Brothers, 1957), 206–207.

4. St. John of Damascus, *On the Divine Images*. I:16. Quoted in Myroslaw Tataryn, "The Eastern Tradition and the Cosmos," *Sobornost*, Vol. 11, Nos. 1–2 (1989), 49.

5. Paul Evdokimov, "Nature," *Scottish Journal of Theology*, Vol. 18, No. 1, March 1965, 16.

6. Reprinted with permission from *Carmina Gardelica*, Vol. One, 247, published by Scottish Academic Press, Edinburgh.

7. Ibid., 249.

8. Ibid., 241.

9. A. M. Allchin, *The Living Presence of the Past* (New York: Seabury Press, 1981), 133.

Four

More Modern Times

CREATION THEMES APPEAR IN THE WRITINGS of Continental reformers, but they were distinctly subordinate to the major issues of personal salvation and the redemption of society.

Luther and Calvin: Human Salvation

Human salvation was the paramount issue for Martin Luther; nature was the backdrop against which the drama of sin, grace, and salvation was played out. Luther decided to become a monk while passing through a violent storm, but his writings contain little nature imagery. With characteristic bluntness he wrote, "Our body bears the traces of God's wrath, which our sin has deserved. God's wrath also appears on the earth in all creatures. . . . And what of thorns, thistles, water, fire, caterpillars, flies, fleas, and bedbugs? Collectively and individually, are not all of them messengers who preach to us concerning sin and God's wrath?"[1]

John Calvin's thoughts about nature are likewise episodic. Unquestionably for Calvin, humans dominate the natural order, which is provided for their use. Through providence, Christians claim the rule of God for the governance of life and the social order. Calvin's beliefs gave theological buttressing to the Protestant ethic and the rise of entrepreneurial capitalism. The created order was not a primary theme for Calvin; still, it constitutes a "beautiful theatre" for God's activity: "In every part of the world, in heaven and on earth, [God] has written and as it were engraven the glory of [God's] power, goodness, wisdom and eternity. . . . For all creatures, from the firmament even to the centre of the earth, could be witnesses and messengers of [God's] glory to all."[2]

Donne: The Distinguishing of Seasons

John Donne, the seventeenth-century poet-theologian, states his belief in an incarnational presence of God in the world more clearly. Donne's "Sermon preached at Paul's upon Christmas Day in the Evening, 1624" unites time, places, seasons, and divinity in a poetic expression of the Incarnation. It is one of the most complete statements of creation spirituality in Chrisian writings anywhere:

> GOD made Sun and Moon to distinguish seasons, and day, and night, and we cannot have the fruits of the earth but in their seasons: But God hath made no decree to distinguish the seasons of [God's] mercies; In paradise, the fruits were ripe, the first minute, and in heaven it is alwaies Autumne, his mercies are ever in their maturity. . . . If some King of the earth have so large an extent of Dominion, in North, and South, as that [God] hath Winter and Summer together in [God's] Dominions, so large an extent East and West, as that [God] hath day and night together in [God's] Dominions, much more hath God mercy and judgement together: [God] brought light out of darknesse, not out of a lesser light; [God] can bring thy Summer out of Winter, though thou have no Spring; though in the wayes of fortune, or understanding, or conscience, thou have been benighted till now, wintred and frozen, clouded and eclypsed, damped and benummed, smothered and stupified till now, and God comes to thee, not as in the dawning of the day, not as in the bud of spring, but as the Sun at noon to illustrate all shadowes, as the sheaves in harvest, to fill all

penuries, all occasions invite [God's] mercies, and all times are [God's] seasons.[3]

Traherne: Landscapes of Glory

In all periods, English creation spirituality, like Celtic and Orthodox writings on this subject, strongly link God and creation. William Blake, Gerard Manley Hopkins, and William Wordsworth are representative names. One of the most complete exemplars of this tradition is a lesser-known cleric-poet, a Herefordshire shoemaker's son and Oxford graduate, Thomas Traherne, (1637–1674). Traherne, known to specialists of the period, now enjoys a larger audience through the work of a contemporary writer on English spirituality, A. M. Allchin.[4]

The seventeenth-century poet's work reflects a childlike joy in creation and a Franciscan view of the symbiotic relationship of all creation. His work is rich and at times repetitious, mainly because Traherne describes a continual interaction between God and creation. Traherne writes,

> You never enjoy the world aright, till you see how a sand exhibiteth the wisdom and power of God and prize in every thing the service which they do you in manifesting [God's] glory and goodness to your soul far more than the visible beauty of their surface. . . .
>
> Your enjoyment of the world is never right till every morning you awake in heaven, see yourself in your Father's palace and look upon the skies and the earth and the air, as celestial joys, having such a reverend esteem of all, as if you were among the angels. . . . Can you take too much joy in your Father's works? [God] is . . . in every thing.[5]

Traherne describes a transfigured world. His work is representative, not exceptional, in the historic tradition of English spirituality. It answers the arguments raised by Simone Weil's probing question: "How can the church call itself catholic if the universe is left out?"

John Wesley: Animal Redemption

John Wesley (1703–1791), in a sermon called "The General Deliverance," uses passages from Romans 8 and Revelation 21 in a bold statement about animal redemption:

> In the new earth, as well as the new heavens, there will be nothing to give pain, but everything that the wisdom and goodness of God can create to give happiness. As a recompence for what they once suffered, while under the "bondage of corruption," when God has "renewed the face of the earth," and their corruptible body has put on incorruption, they shall enjoy happiness suited to their state, without alloy, without interruption, and without end.

Like many writers in recent times, Wesley sees Romans 8 as a text extending to animal life as well as human beings:

> While [God's] creatures "travail together in pain," [God] knoweth all their pain, and is bringing them nearer and nearer to the birth, which shall be accomplished in its season. . . . [The end for such creatures is] not by annihilation; annihilation is not deliverance. . . .
>
> Nothing can be more express: away with vulgar prejudices, and let the plain word of God take place. They "shall be delivered from the bondage of corruption into glorious liberty,"—even a measure, according as they are capable,—of "the liberty of the children of God."
>
> To descend to a few particulars: the whole brute creation will then, undoubtedly, be restored, not only to the vigour, strength, and swiftness which they had at their creation, . . . but to a degree of it as much higher than that, as the understanding of an elephant is beyond that of

a worm. And whatever affections they had in the garden of God, will be restored with vast increase; being exalted and refined in a manner which we ourselves are not now able to comprehend. The liberty they then had will be completely restored, and they will be free in all their motions. . . . No rage will be found in any creature, no fierceness, no cruelty, or thirst for blood. So far from it, that "the wolf shall dwell with the lamb, the leopard shall lie down with the kid; the calf and the young lion together; and a little child shall lead them" (Isaiah 6.6).

Wesley adds a final paragraph, sharply qualifying his comments—like a preacher looking at a sermon and asking, "Did I go too far?" He says, "But though I doubt not that the Father of All has a tender regard for even [the] lowest creatures, and that, in consequence of this, [God] will make them large amends for all they suffer while under their present bondage; yet I dare not affirm that [God] has an *equal regard* for them and for the children of [humanity]. . . . God regards [the] meanest creatures much; but [God] regards [humanity] much more."[6]

Wesley's preoccupations were preaching salvation and organizing the church. He was deeply aware of cruelty to animals but otherwise does not comment extensively on creation issues. His journals contain entries that merit a place among the most vivid and best examples of English eighteenth-century travel writings.

Francis Kilvert: Imagery of New Life
What is most interesting about English creation spirituality is that, once the search for it begins, sources multiply, bridging centuries and authors of poetry, sermons, and diaries; greater and lesser known figures. Francis Kilvert was a young curate in a Welsh parish, whose chronicle of rural people, their practices, and the change of seasons resemble Constable paintings. His lengthy diary, filled with imagery of new life, describes Easter Eve and Easter Day in a rural village in 1870: "I awoke at 4:30 and there was a glorious sight in the sky, one of the grand spectacles of the Universe. . . . I

got up soon after 5 and set to work on my Easter sermon getting two hours for writing before breakfast."

On Easter Eve Kilvert sees school children gathering flowers and moss, Mrs. Morrell decorating the baptismal font, and a stream of villagers in the late afternoon coming to dress the graves with flowers. "The sun went down in glory behind the dingle, but still the work of love went on through the twilight and into the dusk until the moon rose full and splendid. The figures continued to move about among the graves and to bend over the green mounds in the calm clear moonlight and warm air of the balmy evening."

At 8 P.M. the choir members gather to rehearse two Easter anthems, "the young people came flocking in from the graves where they had been at work or watching others working, or talking to their friends, for the Churchyard on Easter Eve is a place where a great many people meet." Moonlight streams in through the chancel windows.

"As I walked down the Churchyard alone the decked graves had a strange effect in the moonlight and looked as if the people had laid down to sleep for the night out of doors, ready dressed to rise early on Easter morning."[7]

Edwin Muir: Creation Spirituality

The English tradition of creation spirituality finds its most complete modern expression in the poetry of Edwin Muir (1887–1959), who spent his youth in Scotland's Orkney Islands and experienced an evangelical conversion in his early years. Deep awareness of the rural landscapes of his childhood and the traditional biblical preaching he was exposed to in Scotland infuses Muir's work. His poem, "The Days,"[8] follows the classic structure of the creation accounts in Genesis 1–2:

> Issuing from the Word
> The seven days came,
> Each in its own place,
> Its own name.

Muir depicts creation's progress in a succession of images common to the Scottish isles:

> The water stirred
> And from the doors were cast
> Wild lights and shadows on the formless face
> Of the flood of chaos.

Muir devotes almost half the poem to the seventh day. Creation progresses—cattle, people, birds, fish, the change from day to night, the activity of winds and waters, and the realization that "this fragmentary day" will pass:

> Into the day where all are gathered together,
> Things and their names, in the storm's and the
>   lightning's nest,
> The seventh great day and the clear eternal weather.

Muir's poem "The Transfiguration," summarizes his Christological vision. At the end of time, all creation praises God. Like writers from Ezekiel to the present, Muir employs a tree image; the Cross becomes once more like the tree that was a central feature of the garden of Eden:

> But he will come again, it's said, though not
> Unwanted and unsummoned; for all things,
> Beasts of the field, and woods, and rocks, and seas,
> And all mankind from end to end of the earth
> Will call him with one voice. In our own time,
> Some say, or at least when time is ripe.
> Then he will come, Christ the uncrucified,
> Christ the discrucified, his death undone,
> His agony unmade, his cross dismantled—
> Glad to be so—and the tormented wood
> Will cure its hurt and grow into a tree
> In a green springing corner of young Eden.[9]

Notes

1. Martin Luther, *Werke Kritische Gesamtausgabe {Schriften}* (Weimar), 42. 155ff., in H. Paul Santmire, *The Travail of Nature: The Ambiguous Ecological Promise of Christian Theology* (Philadelphia: Fortress Press, 1985), 125.

2. John Calvin, *Opera Selecta* 9.793, 795. Cited by Francis Wendel, *Calvin: The Origin and Development of His Thought*, trans. Philip Mamet (New York: Harper & Row, 1963), 34. Quoted in Santmire, *Travail of Nature*, 128.

3. John Donne, in *LXXX Sermons*, 1640, quoted in A. R. Peacocke, *Creation and the World of Science*, (Oxford: Clarendon Press, 1979), 359.

4. A. M. Allchin, ed., *Landscapes of Glory* (Harrisburg, PA: Morehouse Publishing, 1989).

5. Ibid., 20–21.

6. From *Sermons on Several Occasions*, Vol. II, introduction by John Beecham (London: Wesleyan Conference Office, 1874), 281–86, contained in Andrew Linzey and Tom Regan, eds.; *Animals and Christianity: A Book of Readings* (New York: Crossroad, 1988), 101–103.

7. Quoted in E. D. H. Johnson, *The Poetry of Earth* (New York: Athenaeum, 1966), 352–57.

8. Edwin Muir, *Collected Poems* (New York: Oxford University Press, 1965), 208–210.

9. Ibid., 200.

Part III

*Ecology
and the
Church
Today*

Five

Today's World

W HAT DOES THE FUTURE HOLD? At this point, science and
politics intersect. We are at a crossroads; our decisions
to act or to refrain from acting will help determine the
future of our planet.

Policy responses include reduced reliance on fossil fuels,
phasing out the use of environmentally destructive gases, and moving from net global deforestation to net reforestation. The imple-
mentation of these measures can decrease significantly the rates of
global warming and sea-level rise. But even if we take such measures immediately, they cannot prevent some warming from occur-
ring in the next few decades.

The United States has only five percent of the world's population but consumes twenty-five percent of the world's commercial
energy annually. The energy consumption ratio of Americans to the
developing world is one to fifteen. International leaders say
Americans criticize Brazilians for wasting the rain forest at a time
when increased vehicle carbon dioxide emissions from industrialized
countries threaten the ozone layer. A tropical ecologist Thomas E.
Lovejoy writes, "If the wealthiest nation on earth, alone responsible
for 20 percent of the annual increase of carbon dioxide, is not seen
to grapple with reduction of energy consumption, it will be very

hard to expect nations of far less wealth to undertake vital environmental measures."

Lovejoy goes on to say, "If we fail on that front, we give credence to accusations of ecological imperialism and the notion of a conspiracy to prevent the poorer nations from their rightful development."[1]

Minorities and the Poor

Minorities and the poor are among the most vulnerable to environmental problems. Lacking resources and mobility, they experience environmental degradation and its human consequences first and most intensely. Population explosions are most evident in urban cities and outlying lands extending from large cities. Sea rise and global warming will register a demonstrable impact on such population concentrations; as will air, water, and soil pollution, the accumulation of garbage, toxic waste, and environmental destruction. With no easy recourse to justice, inadequate health, educational, sanitation, and environmental conditions will first affect the poor and minorities. The loss of topsoil, desertification, and the destruction of rain forest will affect most dramatically those who live closest to the land, the poor. Environmental degradation impacts on human personality.

As an idyllic landscape lightens the spirit, an urban wasteland takes its toll on inhabitants' personalities. A well-known photographer of the earth, Ansel Adams, feels that the influence surrounding the first three or four years of life determines a child's direction in years to come. The coming generations will suffer for our embezzlement of resources. Seeing and knowing the natural world, better equips our children to face the realities of life. Only then will our children come to realize the noble potentials of existence that earth has to offer.

Thomas Berry, well known for his religious writings on ecology, tells us that we do not face extinction but degradation. For Berry, degradation is worse than extinction because the next generation will have to live among the ruins of the natural world and the industrial world.

Humanity faces a global challenge. Humans are not bystanders in the emergence of a global problem. We are the problem's cause, and we can provide a solution. Solving the problem requires a new global consciousness: the political and religious equivalent of the view of Planet Earth from space. Those who wrestle with global environmental problems can profit from the remarks of a Syrian astronaut, Muhamed Ahmad Farsis, "From space I saw earth—indescribably beautiful with the scars of national boundaries gone."[2]

The comments from space of three other astronauts illustrate the new, hope-filled perspective on Earth, a challenge to apply Paul's creation vision in a planetary context:

The first day or so we all pointed to our countries. The third or fourth day we were pointing to our continents. By the fifth day we were aware of only one earth. (Sultan Bin Salman Al-Saud, Saudi Arabia)

It isn't important in which sea you observe a slick of pollution, or in the forests of which country a fire breaks out, or on which continent a hurricane arises. You are standing guard over the whole of our earth. (Yuri Artyukin, the Soviet republics)

As I looked down, I saw a large river meandering slowly along for miles, passing from one country to another without stopping. I also saw huge forests, extending across several borders. And I watched the extent of one ocean touch the shores of separate continents. Two words leaped to mind as I looked down on all this: commonalty and interdependence. We are one world. (John-David Bartoe, USA)[3]

Nothing less than a biblical understanding of creation that extends beyond our immediate orbits to include the biosphere and its God-given contents will equip us to face the global environmental crisis.

At the same time, we need to reorder perceptions of our history, understandings that have allowed us a vision of earth as an endless cornucopia that will tolerate our abuse and still be constantly fruitful.

In recent American history, interpretations of the biblical creation stories support visions of open frontiers and ceaseless agricultural production. We fuse Genesis and the Frontier thesis. We follow that thinking with the New Frontier and outer space as frontier extensions. We envision a picture postcard world of amber waves of grain and alabaster cities set against purple mountains.

Once we settle the land, the plow that broke the plain leads to new bounty. Passenger pigeons and wild buffalo are there to be shot from moving trains. A frontier exegete said it was fine to shoot passenger pigeons; it was like God's giving the wandering Hebrews quail for food. Dominion over the earth meant limitless exploitation.

This basic lack of balance with the world around us arises from a fundamental absence of equilibrium within us. Failure to reconcile the violence and angry contradictions within us helps explain violence toward the physical universe and animals. Photo essays of environmental destruction in Eastern Europe and parts of the United States are like depictions of World War II bombing raids or battle scenes. They recall a passage from the prophet Hosea:

> Therefore the land will be desolate
> and all who live in it will languish,
> with the wild beasts and the birds
> of the air;
> even the fish will vanish from the sea (4:3).

Apocalypse Now

News photos and television clips chronicle our troubled relationship with our planet. An Alaskan shore bird flaps an oil-sogged wing hoping to rise above the stony coast. A majestic lion races briefly ahead of the low-flying helicopter. A hunter will gun it down with an automatic rifle. A native Brazilian forest dweller cuts into the diminishing rain forest to clear a farming plot. Cars on a Los Angeles freeway send carbon emissions skyward. A garbage scow sails from port to port, seeking a welcome harbor for rotting debris.

The range of environmental issues flashes before us. Scientists and policy makers debate the data and needed remedies. They are driven by a realization that time is running out for many species and does not favor the controlling agent, humanity. Antagonisms develop between those ancient stock characters "business" and "do-gooders." "Big government" assumes a ponderously cautious mediator's role. All participants must bring true leadership and enlightened cooperation.

Major expenditures and job dislocations conflict with ideal solutions. "If they cut down on the use of coal, my daddy is out of a job," an Appalachian child tells a journalist. Preservation of Africa's shrinking elephant herds conflicts with expanding human populations; safeguarding a vanishing owl species in the American northwest may cost loggers' jobs. "Good planets are hard to find," say graffiti scrawled in a park.

A recent film from southern Africa shows the centuries-old migration of desert antelope across a parched region to water and grazing grounds and to have their young. The country's govern-ment stretches a high wire fence along its borders to block migra-tions. The fence is soon piled high with dead antelope carcasses. The creatures can run fifty miles an hour. They follow the barrier for great distances in the hot sun but have no skills to cross the wire fence that keeps them from water.

There is a shot of a proud beast, so thirsty it can no longer walk. As it falls, its movements are graceful; the way a tiring cham-pion athlete still shows traces of grace and motion that once brought crowds to their feet. The antelope raises its head, the village children stone it. The animal makes a last effort to spring up. The rocks rain on it, the struggle ceases, it falls and dies.

Humane society workers in crime-ridden urban American neighborhoods report that crimes of violence against animals fre-quently resemble crimes against humans; i.e. burnings, beatings, and sexual abuse. If animals are objects of deep human affection, they are also voiceless subjects of intense human violence. The poacher who tells the game warden, "I just wanted to see something die" reflects the fullness of what Hannah Arendt calls "the banality of evil."

What do these examples say about humanity's insensitivity toward creation? They suggest that we are exploiting the universe and one another. The sources of this cruelty, indifference, and waste come from deep within ourselves. Thomas Traherne said, "You will never enjoy the world aright, till the sea itself floweth in your veins, till you are clothed with the heavens, and crowned with the stars, and perceive yourself to be the sole heir of the whole world, and more than so, because [others] are in it who are every one sole heirs as well as you."[4]

Chief Seattle Didn't Say It

In a time of the present ecological crisis, we tend to look to the past and project it as an idyllic age of wise people living in harmony with nature. We like to read quotes of native American piety that suggest a hidden world of ecological-spiritual unity. We can find many such statements of indigenous spirituality deeply linked with God and nature, but we must use them with caution. No generic American Indian position on creation spirituality exists any more than does a New England or Asian-American position on the subject exist. We need to know who holds which beliefs, when, and in what context. Anthropologists realize that the same native society that produces sensitive poetry and proverbs about nature can employ slash-and-burn agriculture and other destructive environmental practices, like dynamiting fish, leveling the rain forest, or setting forest fires to drive game toward hunters.

However, traditional societies around the world have lived close to the land, and such societies can contribute to expanded contemporary spirituality. Well-intentioned people, in their eagerness to publicize American Indian beliefs, often do themselves and such societies a disservice by accepting fragments of creation spirituality narratives without placing them in a proper context.

A more discerning perspective would not have given wide-spread publicity to a non-Indian film script, "Chief Seattle's Speech," perhaps the most quoted reference of indigenous belief uttered from American pulpits.[5] Chief Seattle's speech was written in 1970–71 as part of a film script by a University of Texas documentary script writer, Ted Perry, who never claimed the text as a historic document. The film, called *Home*, was shown on national television without an author's credit line. Chief Seattle gained international attention and a place in ecological literature for a discourse he never uttered.

The original Chief Seattle lived in the Pacific Northwest (c. 1786–1866) and signed an 1855 treaty ceding large land holdings to the US. government. His brief remarks, reported thirty years after they were spoken, do not resemble the later words attributed to him. Whatever its poetic merits, "Chief Seattle's Speech" is not a document of native American spirituality and should not be represented as such.

Yet, the contemporary church can learn a great deal about reverence for the earth and its creator, and humanity's important, but limited, place in the cosmos from authentic native spirituality. A Shona proverb reminds us, "The soil is never satisfied; it swallows even important people." Numerous harvest prayers and thanksgivings, and blessings for daily life bear resemblances to Celtic and Orthodox spirituality.

Black Elk, a Lakota Indian and Roman Catholic living in Nebraska, expresses the relationship among deity, humanity, and creation:

> We regard all created beings as sacred and important, for everything has an . . . influence, which can be given to us, through which we may gain a little more understanding if we are attentive. We should understand well that all things are the works of the Great Spirit. We should know that [the Great Spirit] is within all things; the trees, the grasses, the rivers, the mountains and all the four-legged animals, and the winged peoples: and even more

important, we should understand that [the Great Spirit] is also above all these things and peoples.[6]

Manifestations of the divine presence will come from many sources, especially those most cherished by the society. Like many indigenous societies,

> The sacred tobacco pipes of the Plains peoples express in comprehensive synthetic manner all that is most sacred to the people. . . . The pipes, which have long wooden stems and stone bowls, are understood to be an axis joining and defining a path between heaven and earth. . . . In solemn prayer, as each grain of carefully prepared tobacco is placed in the pipe, mention is made of some aspect of creation, so that when the bowl is full it contains the totality of time, space, and all of creation including humankind. . . . Often, in concluding the rite the participants in the communal smoking recite, "We are all related."[7]

In seeing the sacredness of all life, some aboriginal people have a great deal to share with modern societies.

While the impressions of poets, artists, and indigenous peoples help give us perspective on the environmental crisis, we can measure the problem's global impact by appraising the data assembled by scientists about the issue, especially the exponential rise in world population, which drives every aspect of the problem.

Population

Population is at the heart of all environmental issues. The sharp increase in human activity pollutes the air; increasing demands on soil poison the earth, taxing the earth's capacity for renewal. At the time of Christ, the world's population was roughly the size of the United States' population today. World population grew from one to two billion persons in 130 years. In 1830 the world's population was one billion people. The next century added another billion people. At present, the world's population grows by a billion persons every ten years. Most of the growth occurs in countries that are least able to provide health, educational, and economic conditions for a meaningful life for most inhabitants. Today the figure is 5.4 billion. Conservative estimates predict that the world's population will double to over 11 billion persons by the next century's end. Each six seconds eighteen persons are born; each hour there are 11,000 new mouths to feed; each year 95 million people, the population of Mexico, are added to the planet.[8]

Natural responses to overpopulation are environmental degradation, the spread of disease and death, and limited lifestyle opportunities for the living. Population growth rates above two percent a year risk overloading the capacity of many world governments to meet basic human needs. Since 1968, at least 200 million people, mostly children, have perished of hunger and hunger-related illnesses. The vulnerable include children in crowded cities, the elderly, and those prone to heart and respiratory illnesses brought on by pollution.

As population increases, global soil losses in excess of new soil formation are estimated at 24/26 billion tons per year. From 1970 to 1990 farmers lost 480 billion tons of topsoil; the earth's forests diminished by 500 million acres; deserts expanded by 300 million acres. Each year, the world's farmers must grow food for 85 million more people on 25 billion tons less topsoil, roughly the amount covering Australia's wheatlands.[9]

One billion people live in nations with the highest standards of living, access to health care, education, and diet. Another billion people live in absolute poverty. Population grows at 2.4 percent annually in poor countries; the population of these countries will double in twenty-nine years. In rich countries, population growth is 0.6 percent annually, doubling in 120 years.[10]

The biblical writers' world was far less populated and polluted than today's earth. The biblical landscape is one of small villages and vast deserts with a handful of trading cities—not the 8.1 billion people projected to crowd the planet by the year 2025. Water shortage, soil exhaustion, reduced ground water, and stress on natural ecosystems further contribute to the problem.

Coastal flooding and sea rise will affect the most at-risk peoples, those who live in populous coastal cities. Desertification will create millions of additional environmental refugees.

"Lord, you lived in Egypt as a refugee, have compassion on all refugees and strangers." The morning sun sends shafts of light against the cathedral's walls, highlighting a carved African Christus. Outside, the sounds of animals and vehicles fill Gaborone's streets, some of whose occupants are political or environmental refugees. Inside, the small circle of worshipers say the litany with special applicability to Zimbabwe. It is not difficult to picture the Holy Family among the wanderers outside, with life possessions balanced in small parcels carried on sticks. Possibly there are fifteen million political and ten million environmental refugees around the world. The latter are scattered from Chernobyl, meaning "wormwood" in Russian, to Bangladesh, from the drought-ridden Sahel and flood-plagued Himalayan watershed to Louisiana's Petroleum Corridor and New York State's misnamed Love Canal.

The Tragedy of the Commons

In the 1830s, William Forster Lloyd, an amateur mathematician, introduced "The Tragedy of the Commons" as an image of world population problems. It has contemporary relevance. The tragedy, as in a Greek drama, is *hubris*, human pride, the occasion of both human success and downfall. The Commons, as in an English village, is a finite landmass accessible to all, where each family keeps its cattle. As long as the number of cattle and people are within the land's carrying capacity, there is no problem. Wars and disease achieve this end for many years. But if each person decides to increase his or her herd's size gradually, the result is initial individual profit and long-term communal tragedy. The increased livestock pushes the land's limited carrying capacity beyond its bounds, and life support systems collapse.

The solution to the population growth problem can never be simply technical. Garrett Hardin, a biologist who brought "The Tragedy of the Commons" into modern usage, concludes that only a landmark change in human values will help.

> The tragedy of the commons as a food basket is averted by private property. . . . But the air and waters surrounding us cannot readily be fenced, and so the tragedy of the commons as a cesspool must be prevented by different means, by coercive laws or taxing devices that make it cheaper for the polluter to treat his [or her] pollutants than to discharge them untreated. . . .
>
> The pollution problem is a consequence of population. It did not much matter how a lonely American frontiersman disposed of his waste. "Flowing water purifies itself every 10 miles," my grandfather used to say, and the myth was near enough to the truth when he was a boy, for there were not too many people.[11]

Water

As population grows, so do demands on the earth's atmosphere and ecosystem. The atmosphere covers all nations and, as a major component of the earth's ecosystem, constantly interacts with oceans, lands, animals, plants, and soils. The ecosystem controls the world's supply of fresh water, food from the sea, the mix of atmospheric gases, crop pollination, pest control, and the delicate mix of forest products. To tamper with the ecosystem is to court serious disruption of planetary stability, including the place of humans in the global economy.

"The Fight for the Water Hole," Frederic Remington's painting, provides an apt metaphor about a contemporary environmental problem—shrinking world water supplies. In the well-known painting, Indians and settlers face each other with drawn rifles around a small pool under the hot desert sky. Water problems are now global political problems. An issue in the 1967 Arab-Israeli war was access to the Jordan River. The waters of 120 of the world's 200 major river systems flow through two or more countries. Eighteen countries drop sewage and other pollutants into the Mediterranean, Homer's wine-dark sea. Israel consumes five times as much water as it neighbors per capita and may have a serious water shortage by the century's end. In the film "Chinatown," the central issue is water rights for a growing Los Angeles. Recently, an expanding Las Vegas discovered it is running out of water and began legal proceedings for water rights in less populated neighboring states. Farmers voice their resistance: "Why should we give up our water to fuel your growth?" In California's San Joaquin Valley, aquifers pump 500 billion gallons a year more than is being replenished.

International tensions could heighten with reduced river flows between Pakistan and India (the Indus) and India and Bangladesh (the Ganges). Regional disputes have occurred in the basins of the Nile, Tigris/Euphrates, Mekong and Rio de la Plata rivers. The possibility of drought-induced conflict is real, given expanding world population and widespread regional water shortages. In the foreseeable future, contests for water may rival disputes for oil in international relations.[12]

The Ozone Layer

A dramatic, human-caused loss of ozone high above the Antarctic alters the globe's atmosphere harmfully. The ozone layer is a thin protective layer of three-molecular oxygen, which shields the globe and its inhabitants from biologically harmful ultraviolet radiation. During the 1970s, some scientists believed supersonic aircraft exhaust gases damaged the ozone layer. But humans, not aircraft, are the great disrupters, chiefly through the discharge of millions of tons of chlorofluorocarbon (CFC) gases into the atmosphere. CFCs cool refrigerators, propel spray cans, and are solvents and staples in the production of foam packing material and styrofoam cups.

For several decades, CFCs represented cheap, safe, and efficient industrial chemicals. What the world didn't realize was that CFCs released chlorine and bromine gases into the atmosphere. Such chemicals have a long life, often more than 100 years, and voracious appetites for ozone. CFCs are among the leading contributors to global warming.

Ozone layer depletion is most evident over the Antarctic, because winter weather conditions there last from April to October. The isolated air circulation encourages low stratospheric temperatures, generating a thin cloud layer. The cold and cloud cover favor the release of chlorine gas in the stratosphere when sunlight reappears in the spring. Chlorine reacts with ozone, destroying nearly half of it in a few weeks. The more chlorine in the atmosphere, the quicker the ozone layer is destroyed.

Reports from World Meteorological Organization Global Ozone Observing System stations in Antarctica confirm a ten-year trend of a loss of about twenty-five percent of total ozone during the Antarctic spring. At some levels, the ozone layer was virtually destroyed.

After October, weather conditions change, the circumpolar vortex disappears, cloud cover lifts, wind exchange with lower latitudes intensifies, and the ozone layer reaches nearly normal values. The Antarctic seasonal observations demonstrate the consequences of human activity on the atmosphere and possible repercussions on the biosphere.

If the ozone layer is to return to something like its natural state, the upper atmosphere's chlorine level must be restored to its premid-1970 level. Atmospheric concentrations of active chlorine were still manageable by natural processes then, before the increasing industrial use of CFCs.

How can this be done? The options are clear. It will require the phasing out of several classes of industrially produced gases, including chlorine-carrying CFCs. Promising substitutes are in production; research laboratories actively seek other replacements.

Through scientific assessments prepared regularly since 1975, governments are aware of the problems, as are industry and citizens' groups. In 1987, a Montreal Protocol was signed by producing countries. It required a fifty percent reduction in CFC production by 1998; in June 1990 a London conference of the same signatories agreed to phase out all CFCs by the year 2000.

Global Warming

An increase in carbon dioxide and other atmospheric gases, caused largely by industrial gases and increased numbers of vehicles and their pollutants, is contributing to a gradual increase in the earth's surface temperature. Sunlight enters the earth's atmosphere, but a small quantity of "greenhouse gases" restrict the escape of infrared radiation, keeping the earth warmer than it would be otherwise. Over the past 160,000 years, until 1800, concentrations of atmospheric carbon dioxide and methane were under 290 parts per million (ppm). Today those concentrations are 354 ppm. More than half that increase occurred since 1950. Using advanced climate models, scientists predict a global mean temperature of about one degree centigrade above 1990 levels by 2025. By 2090, average temperatures may increase by 3°C globally, within a range of 2° to 5°C. The earth will be warmer than at any time in the past 150,000 years.[13]

The physical and biological world, the setting for human political and economic activity, is experiencing significant change. Scientists suggest the possibility of agriculture's being affected, particularly in vulnerable regions least able to adjust. These include Brazil, Peru, the African Sahel, Southeast Asia, the Asian region of the Soviet republics and China. On the other hand, it is possible that high and midlatitudes of the Northern Hemisphere will experience extended growing seasons.

Relatively small climate change can cause water resource problems, especially in arid and semiarid regions of Africa and humid places where demand or pollution has led to water scarcity. Regions dependent on unregulated river systems, such as Southeast Asia, are particularly vulnerable to water resource change.

Global warming will accelerate sea-level rise, modify ocean circulation, and change marine ecosystems, with socioeconomic consequences. These consequences will compound problems of crowded coastal regions, like population and overharvesting. A one-meter water rise by the year 2100 would leave some island countries of the Caribbean and Asian Pacific uninhabitable and make environmental refugees out of tens of millions of people. It will threaten low-lying urban areas; flood productive land; contaminate fresh water supplies; and overtax public safety, health, housing, and other thinly spread governmental services.

The most vulnerable populations are in developing countries, among the poorest of the poor, especially in the world's growing megacities. Many such cities are in tropical zones, already exposed to natural hazards like flooding, drought, landslides, severe windstorms, and tropical cyclones.

Desertification

Desertification, the gradual loss of cropland and pasturage, is not an abstract word. During a recent visit to Chad, a landlocked central African country, I heard people from several ethnic groups discuss its effects with the same hesitation and puzzlement they would use if the words were *cancer* or *AIDS*. The Sahara is moving slowly south, pushed by years of drought and the loss of pastures. With the loss of grazing land, plants whose roots held soil in place also go. The systematic felling of trees for firewood, the main energy source for ninety percent of people in much of subsaharan Africa, also results in soil loss.

The desert's southern march in turn triggers social change. For example, nomads must alter traditional migratory patterns and they and their camels intersect with cattle raisers as both move toward scarce pasturage and wells. Traditionally, such societies spend most of the year dispersed in small bands, wandering with animals in search of grazing land. When the rains begin, they move toward a common point to sell cattle, visit one another, hold marriages, and affirm clan solidarity through common meals, long conversation, and gift exchanges. Such times are shorter and poorer now as the nomads devote more energy to finding food for humans and animals. Some nomadic societies are decomposing as strongly individualistic desert people seek work in crowded cities. Groups of cattle raisers, whose herds once passed seasonally through the more densely populated southern farmlands, now settle there. This settlement creates the classic farmer-cattle raiser conflicts of the American West.

I asked a French demographer, "What is Chad's present population, and what will it be a generation from now?"

"Six million now, eighteen to twenty-four million in thirty to forty years," he replied, "allowing for a twenty percent decrease in live births."

Peasant attitudes aid desertification. They consume firewood for food preparation and for heat. Bottled gas is prohibitively expensive. To drive animals toward hunters, peasants often burn off large sections of dried bush, destroying topsoil and pasturage. A common saying is, "It's all right to go into the interior and take what you need, nature will do the rest."

Religious leaders, like Chad's government leaders, show marginal interest in environmental problems. I told a local pastor how many western countries are beginning to link environmental and religious interests. When I mentioned the Blessing of the Animals service on Saint Francis's Day in October, he laughed merrily, "If we did that here, it would take us several days."

On my last day in N'Djamena, the capital, I bought a set of biblical postcards done in local settings. In one, Jesus stood in a slender African wooden fishing boat, its inhabitants looking at him with amazement. The text was, "Who can this be? Even the wind and the sea obey him" (Mark 4:41). The local landscape looked like nearby Lake Chad after a storm.

I thought of that text, which Christian ecologists often use to link Christ with nature. Thus far, not many Africans connect their religion with environmental responsibility. Problems of survival and earning a living take precedence. There is a paradox here: Africans live close to the land and are sensitive to its poetry, but not many move beyond the poetry to save the land.

Forests and Biodiversity

Forests everywhere are shrinking visibly. What was once a seemingly limitless resource is now scarce. The "trees in the countryside [that] will clap their hands" (Is. 55:12) are increasingly fewer. The earth loses approximately 17 million hectares of tropical forest annually. Lester Brown's 1991 Worldwatch report estimates 1.5 billion hectares of primary forest remain out of 6.2 billion that existed before the beginning of settled agriculture. Half that land was logged for timber, the rest disappeared as the number of land speculators, peasant farmers, and loggers increased.[14]

The Pacific Northwest timber industry will decline as loggers eliminate old-growth forests. Meanwhile, the number of countries exporting tropical wood has dropped. The main causes of primary forest destruction in the Northern and Southern Hemispheres are industrial timber cutting and land clearing for farming. Logging in the tropics, for example, consumes about 4.5 million hectares of rain forest each year. Deforestation leads to soil erosion and the loss of plant and animal life. Nigeria, once a major timber exporter, spent $100 million on forest product imports in 1988, while earning only $6 million from timber exports. The significant timber holdings of other countries, like Ghana and the Ivory Coast, are nearly exhausted. A well-known biologist frames the question:

> Why should we care? What difference does it make if some species are extinguished, if even half of all the species on earth disappear? Let me count the ways. New sources of scientific information will be lost. Vast potential biological wealth will be destroyed. Still undeveloped medicines, crops, pharmaceuticals, timber, fibers, pulp, soil-restoring vegetation, petroleum substitutes, and other products and amenities will never come to light. It is fashionable in some quarters, to wave aside the small and obscure, the bugs and weeds, forgetting that an obscure moth from Latin America saved Australia's pasture land from overgrowth by cactus . . . that the bark of the Pacific yew offers hope for victims of ovarian and breast cancer, that a chemical from the saliva of leeches dissolves blood clots during surgery, and so on down a roster already grown long and illustrious despite the limited research addressed to it.[15]

Tropical forests provide foods, essential oils, and commercial products like latexes. Dr. Mark Plotkin of Conservation International observed the following: "Most every major commodity in the international market place was first discovered by native peoples. An American breakfast, from cornflakes and bananas, to coffee, sugar, and orange juice and even hash brown potatoes, is all based on foods that originated in the tropics."[16]

Dr. Michael Balick of the New York Botanical Garden said, "Of more than 265,000 known plant species, less than one percent have been tested for medical applications. Yet out of this tiny portion have come twenty-five percent of medicines."[17]

Humanity is only beginning to measure the mystery of biodiversity in forest regions. Millions of wild species have not been cataloged and tested at a time when species' loss proceeds in an exponential manner. Some West African plants produce proteins infinitely sweeter than sucrose. Possibly twenty species provide ninety percent of the world's food at present, while perhaps 30,000 species of plants contain edible parts. A wild Amazonian palm provides the world's highest known yield of vegetable oil. Amazon turtles are an excellent source of meat at considerably less cost and ecological devastation than is caused by cattle. Mass-produced saplings give pulp and fiber easily. The rosy periwinkle from Madagascar, an easily overlooked plant, offers the cure to two deadly cancers: Hodgkin's disease and acute lymphocytic leukemia. Drug sales of these two substances exceeds $180 million a year.[18]

Native herbalists represent the refinement of centuries of trial-and-error experimentation. As the loss of certain key species reflects the collapse of ecosystems, the dwindling number of herbalists mirrors the vanishing of long-established cultures. Most such healers are elderly now, and their knowledge dies with them. Younger people are uninterested in lengthy apprenticeships; they prefer modern medicine or are influenced by electronic media. Little more than a decade remains to preserve traditional herbalists' knowledge of rain forest cures. The Pulitzer prize-winning biologist Edward O. Wilson has written,

The ethical imperative should therefore be, first of all, prudence. We should judge every scrap of biodiversity as priceless while we learn to use it and come to understand what it means to humanity. We should not knowingly allow any species or race to go extinct. And let us go beyond mere salvage to begin the restoration of natural environments, in order to enlarge wild populations and stanch the hemorrhaging of biological wealth. There can be no purpose more inspiring than to begin the age of restoration, reweaving the wondrous diversity of life that still surrounds us.[19]

Notes

1. Thomas E. Lovejoy, "The Third World's Environment: A Global Dilemma," *EPA Journal*, July/ August 1989.

2. "Report of the American Bar Association Inter-Generational Accords on the International Law of the Environment," Tort and Insurance Practice Section (Chicago, Ill.: American Bar Association, 1990), 25.

3. Ibid., 6.

4. A. M. Allchin, ed., *Landscapes of Glory* (Harrisburg, PA: Morehouse Publishing, 1989), 21.

5. Rudolf Kaiser, "Chief Seattle's Speech(es): American Origins and European Reception," in Brian Swann and Arnold Krupat, eds., *Recovering the Word: Essays on Native American Literature* (Berkeley: University of California Press, 1987), 497–536.

6. Quoted in Joseph Epes Brown, *The Spiritual Legacy of the American Indian* (New York: Crossroad, 1982), 38–39.

7. Ibid, 17.

8. I am grateful to Ambassador Marshall Green, a director of the Population Crisis Committee and former U.S. Ambassador to Australia and Indonesia, and Assistant Secretary of State for East Asian Affairs, for providing basic data on the relationship among population, the environment, and public policy issues. This distinguished diplomat and foreign policy expert has spent some of the most productive years of his long career calling public and governmental attention to these crucial problems as a new dimension in foreign affairs.

9. Paul R. Ehrlich and Anne H. Ehrlich, *The Population Explosion* (New York: Simon and Schuster, 1990).

10. Ibid.

11. Garrett Hardin, "The Tragedy of the Commons," *Science*, Vol. 162, 13 December 1968, 1243–48.

12. Erlich, *Population Explosion*, 172.

13. J. T. Houghton, G. J. Jenkins, and J. J. Ephraums, eds., *Climate Change*, The IPCC Scientific Assessment (Cambridge: Cambridge University Press, 1990).

14. Sandra Postel and John C. Ryan, "Reforming Forestry," in Lester R. Brown, *State of the World, 1991* (New York: W.W. Norton, 1991), 74–92.

15. Edward O. Wilson, *The Diversity of Life* (Cambridge, MA: The Belknap Press of Harvard University, 1992), 346–47.

16. Daniel Goleman, "Shamans and Their Lore May Vanish with Forests," in "Science Times," *The New York Times*, 11 June 1991, 6.

17. Ibid.

18. Wilson, *Diversity of Life*, 282–284, 293–295.

19. Ibid., 351.

Six

The World We Seek

INTERNATIONAL RELATIONS HAS CHANGED ITS EMPHASIS in recent years. Until lately, political science textbooks would not have included population growth, deforestation, transboundary air pollution, and global climate change as subjects of international statecraft. As the Cold War recedes, such scientific questions replace the Soviet-American confrontation as issues in international relations.

Providing basic food and services will devour capital. Transportation, clean water, health care, and urban support systems will struggle to keep pace with growth. Human rights and access to justice may suffer as the quality of life is threatened and authoritarian, centralized governments apply quick fixes to long-term problems. Some of those most affected, like the atmosphere, animals and birds, the land and sea, rivers and deserts, cannot speak for themselves. We will cast advocates for diminished population growth, a judicious conservation of resources, and modest lifestyles as prophets and iconoclasts. Still, the problem is before the earth in its urgency and complexity. Damning the messenger or quarreling with the message will not make it go away. How can we find a framework that allows business, government leaders, scientists, and ordinary citizens from the Northern and Southern Hemispheres to find common ground to solve the problem of safeguarding the future of life on earth?

Albert Schweitzer, missionary, musician, and Nobel Prize winner, felt that a person's religion was of little value unless even seemingly insignificant creatures benefited from it. For a truly religious person, all of life is sacred.

Recently a beloved dog, a pet of nine years, died, leaving memories; and as visible traces, only a frayed collar, chewed tennis ball, and battered pan. How different that is compared to the 1,200 pounds of waste each American generates on an average annually and leaves as a signature in our habitat.

An African archaeologist described his students' joy in finding a long-abandoned village's garbage pit; from a few square yards of remains they could sketch the profile of a vanished culture. Suppose an archeological team explored most cities' garbage dumps. What story would our garbage tell? Waste material experts say it is difficult to dispose of tons of hardly-used telephone directories each year. They accumulate and do not biodegrade easily. And each year, Americans discard 1.1 million tons of disposable plates and cups, enough to set a picnic for everyone in the world six times over.

Part of our religious response comes through changed, simpler, less wasteful lifestyles. The reordering of national priorities on the use of energy and more thoughtful stewardship of the natural resources entrusted to us is also an issue. A Methodist study asks the following question: "What is the future of the earth to be? . . . We cannot presume that if we abuse it to the utmost God will interrupt our folly and somehow preserve us. But we believe that in the ultimate time of God the whole creation will come to fulfil his will, obtain the glorious liberty of the children of God, and all things be made new. By that trust we live and pray and worship, and find the strength to sustain the whole long struggle to obey God's commands."[1]

The present crisis has scientific, political, and religious dimensions. A well-known Australian biologist and Templeton prize winner, Charles Birch, wrote, "Total spiritual confusion prevails in the modern world about the relationship of humanity to nature in a technological culture. Churches and theologians, intimidated by secular culture, leave the task to others. . . . The whole of creation cries out in agony for liberation. . . . Can religions remain silent on this agony any longer?"[2]

We need new metaphors and a synthesis of scientific, humanistic, and religious thought to understand the environmental crisis. The fragile biosphere, with 1.4 million named and more than 5 million unnamed species, undergoes constant metamorphosis. Still, humanity inaccurately regards nature as constant and unchanging. This view comes from our uncritical acceptance of an earlier mechanistic view of the universe's working like a watch, wheel, gearbox, or engine. While we retired such theological deism to library back shelves long ago, equally dated metaphors remain in modern-day environmental discourse.

The problem is finding new symbolic language into which emerging scientific data fits. Joseph Campbell correctly observes, "Science itself is now the only field through which the dimensions of mythology can be again revealed."[3] The biosphere is open to scientific analysis and to a new kind of understanding because of new knowledge and new metaphors. A delicate network of constantly transforming organisms of many species and environments sustains life. Living and nonliving parts cycle the energy flow and chemical elements that support life.

What are the new environmental metaphors? The first color shots of "spaceship earth," a fragile planet, our island home, transformed human perceptions of nature. Botkin suggests the computer and the spaceship provide root images for explaining nature. Both images have merit, yet pose problems. The computer can absorb new and changing information and can correct for ambiguity and discordant data, but computers have no life of their own.

The spaceship is a limited metaphor as well since omniscience above the earth does not explain who is monitoring the dials and turning the knobs. "We need to instrument the cockpit of the biosphere and let up the window shade so that we begin to observe nature as it is, and not what we imagine it to be."[4]

A careful study of the biblical accounts of creation, the Flood, Job, and the Psalms discloses a world of violent, random change. Likewise, New Testament concepts of Incarnation, Atonement, Crucifixion, Resurrection, and Paul's understanding of the whole creation's struggling, as with birth pangs, offer ways of viewing creation's unfolding drama and how humans can respond intelligently to change.

Science will provide the data on its dimensions; politicians and interest groups will seek solutions; religiously sensitive people will see the problem in its totality. Many persons will accept the idea that creation comes from God and was given to humanity for use during a brief passage on earth. We can see the loving presence of God in the world, in plants, animals, and people; or we can exploit them indiscriminately with awful consequences. The biblical record from Old to New Testament times chronicles the sweep of humanity's relationship with its Creator.

Nature is the stage, often the battleground, where we play out this drama. The picture is not a long symmetrical mural. It is a canvas filled with individual manifestations of the divine presence or demonic consequences of the misuse of creation. To the scientists and policy makers, add the insights of poets and prophets, those solitary figures who point toward the world that might be if we will heed a deeper call and reorder our lives. An English Methodist writer states,

> The new covenant holds good. The energizing power of the Holy Spirit is given us. This should encourage all Christians to help create the new political will which the nations so desperately need, the will to respect nature, heal its wounds, cleanse its pollutions, control the demands made upon it and develop new appropriate lifestyles. Likewise, our technology must be reharnessed, redirected, made to respect nature. We owe this to future generations, and supremely we owe it to God.[5]

In 1961, during a time when civilization focused on nuclear, not environmental, destruction, the American poet Richard Wilbur wrote "Advice to a Prophet." The advice, like that of most prophets, remains timeless:

> When you come, as you soon must, to the street
>   of our city,
> Mad-eyed from stating the obvious,
> Not proclaiming our fall but begging us
> In God's name to have self-pity,
>
> . . . .
>
> What should we be without
> The dolphin's arc, the dove's return.
>
> These things in which we have seen ourselves
>   and spoken?
> Ask us, prophet, how we shall call
> Our natures forth when that live tongue is all
> Dispelled, that glass obscured or broken
>
> In which we have said the rose of our love and
>   the clean
> Horse of our courage, in which beheld
> The singing locust of the soul unshelled,
> And all we mean or wish to mean.
>
> Ask us, ask us whether with the wordless rose
> Our hearts shall fail us; come demanding
> Whether there shall be lofty or long standing
> When the bronze annals of the oak-tree close.[6]

Biblical prophets are neither optimists nor pessimists but realists, prescribing strong medicine in difficult times. Lester Brown of Worldwatch suggests that for American citizens at least, we need a mobilization of consciousness and action resembling a wartime mobilization. Americans traditionally respond to challenges with altruism, innovation, and energy. Such a time is upon us. If we accept the biblical call to restore God's world, we speak not only of a community and global issue but of making something beautiful for God.

"The heavens are telling the glory of God; and the [earth] proclaims [God's] handiwork," the psalmist says. And in the transfigured Christ, past and present unite, nature and humanity converge. The God who placed the power of healing or destruction in human hands, calls us to use creation reverently and responsibly.

During the United Nations Conference on Environment and Development (UNCED) held in Rio de Janerio, Brazil, in June 1992, Sir Shridath Ramphal, former secretary-general of the Commonwealth, said, "Each of us—man, woman and child, rich and poor, of whatever faith, whatever race, whatever religion—must begin to take up our mutual dual citizenship. We must all of us belong, and have a sense of belonging, to two countries—our own and the planet."[7]

One of the final images in Revelation is a redemptive scene that calls humanity to commitment and hope: "the river of the water of life, sparkling like crystal, flowing from the throne of God," and "on either side of the river stood a tree of life, which yields twelve crops of fruit, one for each month of the year. The leaves of the trees are for the healing of the nations" (22:1, 2-3).

Notes

1. "A Discussion Document on Christian Faith Concerning the Environment," *Floods and Rainbows: A Study Guide on the Environment—for Those who Care about the Future* (Methodist Church Division of Social Responsibility: London, 1991).

2. Timothy B. Lynch, "Two Worlds Join to Preserve the Earth," *Christianity and Crisis*, Vol. 50, No. 7, 14 May 1990, 144.

3. Joseph Campbell, *The Masks of God: Primitive Mythology* (New York: Viking, 1959), 468, quoted in Daniel B. Botkin, *Discordant Harmonies: A New Ecology for the Twenty-First Century* (New York: Oxford University Press, 1990), 191.

4. Botkin, *Discordant Harmonies*, 192.

5. *Floods and Rainbows*.

6. Richard Wilbur, "Advice to a Prophet," in *New and Collected Poems* (New York: Harcourt Brace Jovanovich, 1958), 182–83.

7. "Sir Shridath Ramphal Addresses Riocentro Group," *Earth Summit Times* (the NGO newspaper published during the conference), 6 June 1992, 16.

Charm for Bewitched Land

Soil, be well again.
Earth, mother of [all],
Let God fulfill you with food, be ripe
And fruitful and give us life.

ॐ *Poems from the Old English*
Burton Raffel, translator

Glossary

BELOW ARE THE DEFINITIONS OF SOME WORDS used in this text. Most are adapted from the *Oxford English Dictionary*.

biosphere: the part of the world in which life can exist.

creation: the act of bringing the world into ordered existence.

earth: the planet third in order from the sun; the human inhabitants of this planet; the solid matter of the planet.

ecology: the branch of biology dealing with the relationships of living organisms to their surroundings, habitats, and modes of life.

ecosystem: the complex of a community and its environment functioning as an ecological unit in nature.

environment: the complex of physical, chemical and biotic factors, like climate, soil and living things, acting upon an organism, ultimately determining its form and survival.

harmony: agreement, accord, congruity; combining of parts to form a consistent, orderly whole.

litany: an extended prayer with various petitions followed by congregational responses.

nature: a creative and regulative force in the universe; an operating force in the material world or the material world itself; the features and products of the earth as contrasted with those of human civilization.

order: a regular, methodical, or harmonious arrangement of nature; in a wider sense: the condition in which everything is in proper place and performs its proper function.

sin: the willful disobedience of a person or people to God's commandments; humanity's putting itself in the place of God.

universe: the world or earth, especially the abode of humanity and the scene of human activities.

world: the earth with its inhabitants and all created things upon it; the terraqueous globe and its inhabitants.

Part IV

Appendices

Appendix 1

An Action Plan
for Individual Churches

IT WAS A STRONG WINTER RAIN; THE BELTWAY WAS A CIRCLE of four lanes of bumper-to-bumper traffic slowly moving in each direction. Next, the drive was along a winding road into southern Maryland, past shells of rain-soaked half-built housing developments named Sherwood Mews and Lochinvar. Past the few remaining dairy farms in Prince George's County, we headed for a meeting with twenty-five local church leaders who braved the storm to hear about the environment. A folding table spread with pamphlets was set beneath the church's principal decoration, a Taiwan-made woven velvet hanging of the Last Supper.

What can we do? they wanted to know. The discussion moved quickly from theology to practical questions:

∾ What good educational materials are available for congregational use?

∾ How can we develop a Lenten program related to the environment?

∾ What can we do about the polluted river running through the county?

∾ How harmful are nuclear wastes to the environment?

Christian churches are in a unique position to exercise leadership in responding to this crisis. At their most expansive, they always have voiced concern for the whole of society, the whole of humanity.

A point of departure for an action program is the parish, which originally meant a local district or neighborhood. Historically, the English parish was both a religious and a legal unit. Each year, church members walked its bounds during Rogation, the three days before Ascension Day, which was often a time of spring planting. The members surveyed the need for land and building improvements, collected tithes, resolved disputes, and arranged for baptisms and weddings. The day's gospel might be read during the traditional procession at the foot of the most imposing oak within the parish bounds.

The idea of parish is a useful point of departure in responding to the environmental crisis. By exploring the concept of "neighbor," church members look both inwardly at their parish community and outwardly to the world.

Worship, the public prayer of God's people, is the church's central activity. A barometer of a church's interests is what the church includes and excludes from its public prayers. During times of national stress, hymns, prayers, and intercessions make topical reference to parish concerns. The environmental crisis provides an opportunity for launching an action program grounded in prayer.

We find a convergence of mainstream and evangelical, small and large denominations on ecology and creation issues. As in few issues, the line between religion and political action is clear on ecological matters. It will take political, economic, and lifestyle changes to restore creation, and that means hard choices, confrontation, and brokering differing viewpoints, often between antagonists praying to the same God.

If Christians opt out of the political arena, environmental degradation will not lessen. The problem will not solve itself. Christians are caught between a rock and a hard place. Those with a biblically oriented faith can read the scriptures and arrive at a new viewpoint about God's presence in the universe, but intellectual understanding is not enough. Christians must translate insight into action. The incarnational presence of God seeks to redeem all creation, including the political order. Proclaiming the good news is carrying a gospel message directly into the policy arena.

Hubert Humphrey once remarked that action by religious groups made passage of the 1964 Civil Rights Bill possible. It is time now for churches to marshall their energies in support of environmental legislation. Recently, in the middle of a discussion with bankers, lawyers, and real-estate developers over the sale and use of a church-owned, 500-acre tract of choice woodlands in a growing suburban community, I was asked, What is the church's position on this land sale? I said the church's position was to bring the disputing parties together, reconciling differences to the extent possible, and using the land prudently. The economic goal was to make a profit to support its ministries, and at the same time to provide the new development's inhabitants with the opportunity to live a healthy lifestyle while being faithful to preserving the region's ecosystem with its diversity of plant and animal life.

Rarely are such negotiations so clear-cut; we live in a broken world, but each day can contribute to further brokenness or further healing. We may wish for the perfect but are grateful to emerge with the possible. We will only drive others and ourselves to distraction if we seek a vision of a perfect society, which means everyone will agree with our position. Sometimes the choice is between a greater and a lesser good. No distinctly Christian legislative prescription will solve the ecological crisis, but Christians can contribute to its resolution.

No solution is likely without adverse economic consequences for some participants. Local builders may suffer if local land is used up and invading nearby wetlands is the only apparent opportunity for them to continue their trade. Coal miners will lose jobs if cleaner, cheaper forms of energy are found, and loggers cannot continue clearing hill after hill forever in the Pacific Northwest and parts of Maine. The issue is not, and never has been, spotted owl versus loggers, or plants in the Brazilian rain forest versus the march of progress.

The basic issue is about preservation of entire ecosystems because of their diversity and content and their contribution to human life, including medical, agricultural, and recreational uses. The issue is about continuing the diversity of life on this planet. This concern should be paramount in political deliberations; and with that in mind, it should be possible to find ways to sustain development within limits of the ecosystem's carrying capacities.

We must accept the reality of economic losses and dislocations that accompany the industries of logging and coal mining. The root cause is not a single confrontation but the gradual decline of these and other industries, of which the current debate is but a symptom.

Public figures have a responsibility beyond their electorates to defend the human and nonhuman inhabitants of the land and the land itself. I felt the absurdity, yet importance, of making a plea to the land developers on the importance of defending the inarticulate constituency of birds, animals, trees and plants—the earth and its biosphere. There, among the charts, graphs, visual aids, and trappings of a board meeting, memories of walking through the Seaton Belt woods remained with me vividly.

If we are at an eventide of sin and ecological destruction, the divine hope is still for forgiveness and restoration. The darkness of Advent heralds the incarnate light of Christmas; the anguish of Good Friday foreshadows the Resurrection, the Sabbath, and the celestial banquet. Thomas Berry, Roman Catholic priest and writer on ecology, said,

> All human institutions, professions, programs, and activities must be judged by the extent to which they inhibit, ignore, or foster a mutually enhancing human-earth relationship. If we remove the beauty of the natural world, we remove the source of our religions, because we remove the sense of the divine, the mysterious, and the majestic. The universe is working for healing. It wants some kind of rapport with humans. The terminal decade of this century is becoming a moment of grace. This follows a trinitarian model of differentiation, inner articulation, and that everything is absolutely bonded with everything else.[1]

Arthur Miller, the contemporary dramatist, describes the interconnectedness of all nature in *Timebends: An Autobiography*. Watching wild animals in a forest on a winter evening, he writes,

And so the coyotes are out there earnestly trying to arrange their lives . . . not knowing it is my forest, of course. And I am in this room from which I can sometimes look out at dusk and see them warily moving through the barren winter trees. . . . At such moments I do not know whose land this is. . . . In the darkness out there they see my light and pause, muzzles lifted, wondering who I am. . . . I am a mystery to them until they tire of it and move on, but the truth, the first truth, probably, is that we are all connected, watching one another. Even the trees.[2]

Notes

1. Thomas Berry, lecture, Catholic University of America, Washington, D.C., 16 November 1992.
2. Arthur Miller, *Timebends* (New York: Grove Press, 1987), 599.

Appendix 2

Worship Possibilities

IMAGINATIVE WORSHIP RESOURCES ARE AVAILABLE from several denominations, especially in old and new hymns. Many hymnals have an index of Topics and Categories. Look under categories such as the following for appropriate hymns: "Adoration and Praise," seasons of the "Christian Year," "Creation," "Glory," "Gratitude," "Harvest," "Heaven," "Joy," "Light," "Nature," "Peace," "World," "Providence," "Redemption."

The liturgical year, corresponding to the change of seasons, provides many possibilities for introducing ecological themes in a religious context; through sacraments like baptism and the Eucharist, water, bread, and wine are "outward and visible signs" of the holiness and goodness of creation.

In an Advent sermon at St. George's chapel in Windsor, Prince Philip said,

> It is at this lowest point of our year that the Christian church sends out the signal of renewal. Christians are asked to prepare for the coming again of our Savior. As we go into the darkest days of winter, we are encouraged to think of the prospect of nature's regrowth and of our own spiritual rebirth. Advent reminds Christians that there is the hope of spiritual rebirth at Christmas; it should also remind us that humanity is part of the natural order and it is our responsibility to give all life on earth that same chance for renewal and rebirth. It ought to remind us that we have no right to exploit it selfishly and ruthlessly. We are partners with all life on earth and joint beneficiaries of God's gifts of the life-giving air, water,

and soil. It should remind us that God did not make us masters of [God's] creation, [God] expects us to be its guardians.[1]

Advent and Ecology, Resources for Worship, Reflection and Action, edited by Martin Palmer and Anne Nash contains several liturgical prayers and sermons drawn from a BBC radio series and published in 1988 by the International Consultancy on Religion, Education and Culture, 9A Didsbury Park, Manchester Polytechnic, Didsbury Site, Manchester M20 OLH, UK.

ON OCTOBER 4, CHURCHES COMMEMORATE THE LIFE OF FRANCIS of Assisi, the twelfth century Italian saint. No one is more associated with ecological issues historically than Francis, whose "Canticle of the Sun" is one of the fullest expressions of the Christian vision of God's presence in creation. Increasingly, churches are holding a blessing of the animals service, a prototype developed by the Order of St. Francis (Little Portion Priory, Long Island). Worship leaders can conduct the brief service outside the church. Include an opening sentence, such as "Blessed art Thou, O God, Sovereign of the Universe, who hast such as these creatures in Thy world." Sections of a hymn and psalm can follow, such as Psalm 8:5-10. Leaders offer two or three prayers, including the following:

> Hear our humble prayer, O God, for our friends the animals, especially for animals who are suffering; for all that are overworked, and underfed and cruelly treated; for all wistful creatures in captivity that beat against their bars; for all that are in pain or dying; for all that must be put to death. We ask for them all your mercy and pity. Make us true friends of animals and to share in the blessing of the merciful; for the sake of your son, Jesus Christ our Lord.

The officiant then blesses each animal with water saying, "May this ___(name)___ and s(he) who cares for it be blessed in the name of the

Father, Son, and Holy Spirit. Amen." The service concludes with a prayer, a hymn, and a dismissal.

After conducting this service in several parishes, I learned first to hold it outdoors; otherwise, maintaining the peaceable kingdom is not a remote possibility. In downtown churches, children brought stuffed animals, as housing developments did not allow live pets.

Notes

1. Martin Palmer and Anne Nash, eds., *Advent and Ecology, Resources for Worship, Reflection and Action.* Word Wildlife Fund for Nature (WWF) UK, Panda House, Weyside Park, Godalming, Surrey, GU7 1XR UK, 1988, 43–44.

To Mourn Their Passing

- White-necked hawk
- American lobster
- Kavalai forest turtle
- Imperial pheasant
- White whale

A woman stood at a lectern and microphone on the north porch of the National Cathedral. In the distance, I heard her reading into the microphone as a small crowd gathered.

- Big-headed swamp turtle
- New Britain sparrowhawk
- Grey-bellied hawk
- Atlantic sturgeon
- Japanese sea lion

"A Roll Call of Species in Danger of Extinction" was the program. "Richard Block, World Wildlife Fund, United States. Hear the names of species in danger of extinction being read aloud. Noon to 3:45 P.M."

- Cheetah, Africa, Middle East, Iran, Russia
- Lake sturgeon, Canada, USA
- Common sturgeon, Eastern Europe
- Madagascar boa, Madagascar
- Riverain rabbit

A Festival of Creation called for "a partnership between the churches and conservation communities" at Washington National Cathedral. A group performed a fourteenth-century Wakefield

Creation drama at the Cathedral's west end. The ancient chants mixed antiphonally with the reading.

- Aquatic warbler
- Seychelles warbler
- Speckled warbler
- Nihoa warbler
- Hawaii elegant sunbird

I sat in a quiet corner of the north porch. Crowds thinned. The sky was brilliant blue with large white clouds; the air was clean after yesterday's rain.

- Congo peacock
- Israel painted frog
- Yellow-shouldered blackbird, Puerto Rico
- White-breasted guinea fowl, West Africa
- Purple-backed sunbeam, Peru

Each half-hour had a different reader. The cadence of their voices resembled the reading of a litany. Hearing the names of each species, I recalled a similar reading of 58,000 names at the Vietnam War Memorial not far away.

- Siberian crane
- Giant panda, China
- Red panda, Nepal
- Mandarin duck, Nepal to China
- Dwarf wedge mussel, USA

Thirty groups set up booths ranging from the American Forestry Association to the World Wildlife Fund. Panels discussed "Creating a Wildlife Preserve in Your Own Backyard," "Oceans in Peril: Plastic Pollution," and "The Best Way to Raise Animals and Plants."

- West African chimpanzee
- Sloth bear
- Yellow-eyed penguin
- African elephant
- Guadalupe fur seal

Presentations of various kinds abounded: "How Different Religions Think and Pray about Nature and Conservation," a concert of Haydn's "Creation," and an organ recital on themes of creation and conservation that concluded with Saint Francis's *Canticle of the Sun*: "Praise be my Lord God with all his creatures, and especially for our brother the sun, who brings us the day and who brings us the light. O Lord, he signifies to us, Thee!"

- Idaho banded mountain snail, USA
- Nashville crayfish, USA
- Texas cave shrimp, USA
- Indian Yosemite snail, USA
- Wild Bactrian camel

I talked with Canon Michael Hamilton, who worked for a year on the program, one program of several marking the cathedral's completion. Still, I kept returning to the north porch to listen to the rhythmic reading of the species. Each segment began with the words: *Victims include.* I said, "Have mercy upon us" as some names were read aloud.

- Apache trout, USA
- Black dolphin
- Smokey eyed brown butterfly, USA
- Delmarva fox squirrel, USA
- Big thicket emerald dragonfly, USA

Above the north porch is a nativity scene, which was cut in stone when the Cathedral was first built. The Christ child lies in the straw. Mary and Joseph are near, as are shepherds, sheep, and an inquisitive cow. Animals were present at the Incarnation, to warm and to be a source of food for the Christ child. You could feel the warmth of their breath on the baby.

- Utah prairie dog
- Florida panther
- Mountain gorilla
- Nile crocodile
- Madagascar side-necked turtle

(The author wrote this meditation at National Cathedral, Washington, D.C., at a *Celebration of Creation* program.)

A Litany for Preserving the Earth

Praise be to God, Creator of the Universe
Let all creation sing God's praise.

Sun and moon, light and darkness;
Skies and water, atmosphere and biosphere;
Warm winds of dawn, cool winds of evening,
Planets and galaxies, microbes and algae:
Let all creation sing God's praise.

in time of planting,
in time of drought,
in time of harvest,
in time of famine,
We praise you, O God

From sudden storms and prolonged drought,
Loss of shoreline and loss of topsoil.
Save us, O God.

From acid rain and global warming,
From sea rise and poisoned soils.
Save us, O God.

From ozone depletion and greenhouse gases,
Toxic waste and ultraviolet radiation.
Save us, O God.

From destruction of habitat and rain forest,
Misuse of marshlands and coastal waterways.
Save us, O God.

From violence toward all majestic creatures, whales and dolphins, eagles and condors, elephants and lions; from violence toward household and farm animals, and from violence toward one another.
Save us, O God.

The trees of the forest clap their hands,
Mountains and hills dance in your presence,
Grain fields and gardens, great trees and sweeping plains.
Praise you, O God.

Oceans and lakes, rivers and brooks
Deep wells and showers, clouds and storms.
Praise you, O God.

Flocks and herds, stray animals and children's pets;
All captive creatures and all who suffer.
Praise you, O God.

Through Job and Noah,
Through psalmists and prophets,
Through the darkness and earthquake at Calvary,
Through the beauty of the Easter garden.
You call us to repentance, O God.

God of the universe, you placed the earth in our trust; help us to preserve it wisely, to understand dominion as responsible partnership with you, and not senseless exploitation of the world's resources. Save us from greed. Give us the gift of prudent lifestyles; of treasuring the simple gifts of earth; and air, light and water.

Help us to cherish the earth in all its mystery, treasure its fragile beauty, and honor its diversity; help us to turn from the paths of selfishness and destruction; let all creation reflect God's wonder and all creatures, in their own voices, sing God's praise.

We thank you, God, creator and sustainer of life.

Help us to preserve this fragile earth and pass it on in trust to our children.

Each plant and animal, particle and planet, are your gifts to us and exalt you, world without end. Amen

Written for Earth Day at National Cathedral, Washington, D.C., 16 June 1991.

Appendix 3

Resources

UNLESS OTHERWISE STATED, THE FOLLOWING MATERIALS are produced by The Methodist Church, Division of Social Responsibility, 1 Central Buildings, Westminster, London SW1H 9NH, England. Order them from the Methodist Publishing House, 20 Ivatt Way, Peterborough PE3 7PG England.

Resource Papers, Reports, and Workbooks

"Keeping and Healing the Creation," a resource paper issued by the Presbyterian Eco-Justice Task Force, published by the Committee on Social Witness Policy, Presbyterian Church, USA. Obtain it from: The Presbyterian Church, USA, Distribution Management Services, 100 Witherspoon Street, Louisville, KY 40202-1396, DMS# 331-89-101, $4.00. Phone: 1-800-227-2872.

"Restoring Creation for Ecology and Justice," a report adopted by the 202nd General Assembly (1990) of the Presbyterian Church, USA, DMS# 0GA-90-002, $1.50.

"Healing and Defending God's Creation: Hands On! Practical Ideas for Congregations," Presbyterian Church, USA, DMS# 259-91-907. This parish educational workbook contains a model worship service and educational activities for people of every age, plus a Blessing of the Soil, Harvest, and Blessing of the Animals. It includes sections on legislation, public policy, and community involvement.

Floods and Rainbows: A Study Guide on the Environment—for Those Who Care about the Future, Methodist Church, Division of Social Responsibility. This twenty-eight page pamphlet has sections on Bible study, energy, population, consumerism, animal welfare, covenant and hope, and success stories of local churches in action.

"Renewing the Earth: An Invitation to Reflection and Action on Environment in Light of Catholic Social Teachings, a Pastoral Statement of the United States Catholic Conference," Washington, DC. A far-reaching pronouncement that calls humanity stewards and cocreators with God in restoring the earth, itself a sacramental universe. Sections on biblical teaching are followed by Catholic Social Teachings and Environmental Ethics. Available from: Office for Publishing and Promotion Services, United States Catholic Conference, 3211 Fourth St. NE, Washington, DC 20017-1194.

Resource Books

Discovering God's Abundance, 1992. Based on harvest themes and international developmental issues, this anthology is a resource guide for churches. It includes poignant readings from Third World sources.

Love Thy Neighbor, Parish Resources for Faithfulness in Creation, a resource book, describes many liturgical, educational, and community action programs for parishes. It was prepared for the Environment Committee of the Peace Commission, Episcopal Diocese of Washington, DC, by the Reverend Carolyn Tanner Irish. Address: Mount St. Alban, Washington, DC 20016. Copies are $12.95, plus $2.00 postage and handling.

Worship Resources

Speak Up for Tomorrow's World: Ideas for Worship with Suggestions for Harvest Services, One World Week and Other Occasions, 1990. An anthology of readings, prayers, and hymns for church and study group use.

"A Service of Worship on the Theme of Green Discipleship," written by Brian Frost and Dennis Richards. Obtain from Green Discipleship, Flat 3, 35 Buckingham Gate, London, SW1E 6PA. Prayers, readings, and hymns for local church use as a self-contained service.

Rural Life Prayers, Blessings and Liturgies, Victoria M. Tufano, ed., The National Catholic Rural Life Conference, 4625 NW Beaver Drive, Des Moines, IA 50310. It contains a thoughtful collection of prayers and blessings, including a blessing of food providers, animals, fields and flocks, and seeds.

Children's Resources

"Tree Time," an information and activity pack for children's programs, Methodist Church, Overseas Division, 25 Marylebone Road, London, NW1 5JR.

The Lorax, Dr. Seuss, Random House, New York, 1971.

50 Simple Things Kids Can Do to Save the Earth, The Earth Works Group, Andrews and McMeel, Kansas City, MO 1990. This highly recommended volume is tastefully illustrated. It is written for children and adults.

Resources to follow the range of environmental issues

"State of the World Report," written by Lester R. Brown and Associates and published by W. W. Norton & Company, 500 Fifth Avenue, New York, NY 10110. This yearly work is among the most sought-after compendiums on global environmental problems. Topics change each year, but the analysis is timely and provocative. Brown is a leading environmentalist, and Worldwatch Institute magazine and other Institute publications are a good way of staying current on environmental issues. Address: Worldwatch Institute, 1776 Massachusetts Avenue, NW, Washington, DC 20036.

A Directory of Environmental Activities and Resources in the North American Religious Community, The National

Religious Partnership for the Environment, 1047 Amsterdam Ave., New York, NY 10025. This publication comes from the pioneering work on environmental issues of The Very Reverend James Parks Morton, Dean, Cathedral of Saint John the Divine and Dr. Carl Sagan, Professor of Astronomy and Director, Laboratory for Planetary Studies, Cornell University.

Books that Identify the Issues

Discordant Harmonies: A New Ecology for the Twenty-First Century, by Daniel B. Botkin, Oxford University Press, New York, 1990. The author is formerly Professor of Biology and Environmental Studies at the University of California, Santa Barbara. In addition to a discussion of global warming, acid rain, the depletion of forests, and the pollution of the atmosphere and oceans, Dr. Botkin argues that our ability to solve these problems is limited not by our scientific knowledge, but by the age-old myths and metaphors shaping our perceptions of the natural world.

Earth in the Balance: Ecology and the Human Spirit, by Al Gore, Houghton Mifflin Company, Boston, 1992. A lucid survey statement of the environmental problem in all its complexity; including scientific, public policy, and religious dimensions, written by a major figure on national and international environmental concerns. Written for the intelligent general reader.

Essays, poetry, and fiction by Wendell Berry deserve study. A Kentucky farmer and author, Berry's works are too wide-ranging to categorize easily. Titles include *A Continuous Harmony: Essays Cultural and Agricultural*, Harcourt Brace, San Diego, CA, 1975; *The Gift of Good Land: Further Essays Cultural and Agricultural*, North Point Press, San Francisco, 1981, and *What Are People for?*, North Point Press, San Francisco, 1990.

Books with practical program suggestions

Embracing the Earth, Choices for Environmentally Sound Living, by Mark Harris, Noble Press, 1990, Chicago, IL. The book has sections on energy conservation, water use, elimination of toxic substances, and recycling.

Caring for God's World: Creative Ecology Ideas for Your Church, Kristen Kemper, ed., Educational Ministries, Inc., Prescott, AZ, 1991.

2 Minutes a Day for a Greener Planet: Quick and Simple Things Americans Can Do to Save the Earth, by Marjorie Lamb, New York: HarperCollins, 1991.

Creation in Crisis, Responding to God's Covenant, by Shantilal P. Bhagat, Brethren Press, Elgin, IL, 1990. An expert in agriculture and Third World issues, the author is an ordained minister in the Church of the Brethren and that denomination's staff expert for ecology and justice issues. Book sections include "A Christian Understanding of Creation," "Planet Earth," "Human Degradation of Creation," and "The Human Future."

Seven Degradations of Creation, by Calvin B. DeWitt, distributed by the Department of Environmental Stewardship, Evangelical Lutheran Church in America, 8765 West Higgins Road, Chicago, IL 60631-4190. This book is a landmark document among Christian ecologists. DeWitt is Professor of Environmental Studies at the University of Wisconsin-Madison, a prolific author and frequent speaker at conferences on Christianity and ecology. He is also a specialist in environmental science, wetland ecology, and land resources.

"Our Only Home Planet Earth, a Gift from God," Keith L. Ignatius, ed., is a Bible study based on the ecology policy statement of the American Baptist Churches, USA. Order from Ecology and Racial Justice Program, National Ministries, American Baptist Churches, USA; P.O. Box 851, Valley Forge, PA 19482-0851. Three years in preparation, this 1989 statement was adopted by the General Board of the American Baptist

Churches. This seventy-page pamphlet contains the comprehensive policy statement, a six-unit Planet Earth Bible Study guide, and twelve meditations by representative church members. Incorporating both biblical insight and scientific data, this publication is excellent for adult study groups.

Christianity and the Environment: A Collection of Writings, by Art Meyer, Mennonite Central Committee, 21 South 12th St., P.O. Box 500, Akron, PA 17501-0500. A thoughtful fifty-page study by a former high school teacher, focusing on food, hunger, relief, development, and environmental issues. Meyer's personal essay "Why I Am an Environmentalist" is a clear statement of religious belief and scientific understanding.

Periodicals

Buzzworm: The Environmental Journal, 2305 Canyon Blvd. Ste. 206, Boulder, CO 80302. Contains timely features, excellent graphics, a bulletin board of environmental jobs, a calendar of upcoming events, plus listings of environmentally oriented travel.

Earth Ethics: Evolving Values for an Earth Community, Center for Respect of Life and Environment, 2100 L Street NW, Washington, DC 20037. News, features, and book reviews with a religious orientation.

Environment, Helen Dwight Reid Educational Fund, Heldref Publications, 1319 Eighteenth St. NW, Washington, DC 20036-1802.

Daily updates

The Legislative Hotline: (202) 797-6655. Sponsored by the National Wildlife Federation, it contains a frequently updated four-minute recording of environmental news and information on pending legislation. Listeners may obtain additional information on any topic broadcast on the Hotline by calling the NWF: (202) 797-6800.

Econet: Environmental Computer network, Institute for Global Communications, 18 DeBoom St., San Francisco, CA 94107. Lists upcoming conferences and events, pending legislation, action by major environmental groups. Participants may post notices. Available on personal computers with modems.

Television and Audiovisual Resources

Many television programs on the environment exist, and most are available on videotape. Lou Niznik maintains a comprehensive listing of current videotapes for loan or purchase. Contact: Earth Communications, 15726 Ashland Drive, Laurel, MD 20707. Niznik's extensive holdings include a "Christians for the Earth" series.

"Restoring Creation for Ecology and Justice," a fifteen-minute video, presents the ecological crisis as an issue in Christian faith. DMS# 331-90-001, $15.00. The film shows scenes of natural beauty and diversity and what humans are doing to destroy and restore creation. Musical selections include J. S. Bach, "Simple Gifts," and "Will the Circle Be Unbroken." The study guide suggests ways to use this material in either four- or eight-week sessions and provides a focused introduction to ecology as both a public policy and a religious issue.

"Making Peace with the Planet," A tape-slide meditation on the environment, 1988.

Trees Mean Life, an audiovisual packet on tree planting in West Africa, 1991. Based on a lifetime commitment by Methodists and others in village life in West Africa to the restoration of tree cover, this study unit discusses the importance of trees to local life and the deep meaning of their loss.

Organizations

Conservation Directory, a comprehensive directory of environmental groups, published annually by the National Wildlife

Federation, 1400 16th St. NW, Washington, DC 20036-2266. Phone: 1-800-432-6564.

Your Resource Guide to Environmental Organizations, a comprehensive guide to environmental organizations with a commentary on each, John Seredich, ed., Smiling Dolphins Press, Irvine, CA 1991.

Religiously related environmental organizations

The American Association of the Green Cross, 10 Lancaster Ave., Philadelphia, PA 19096-3495. A biblically based ecology action organization created to promote earth-healing. It emphasizes volunteer action.

Earth Ministry, 1305 NE 47th St., Seattle, WA 98105. The Rev. Carla V. Berkedal, former Canon Pastor of St. Mark's Episcopal Cathedral in Seattle, has started this full-time ministry that includes conferences, preaching, and assisting parishes in the organization of creation and ecology programs.

The Evangelical Environmental Network (EEN), 10 Lancaster Ave., Wynnewood, PA 19096. Calls evangelicals to think biblically about God's commands to care for creation as responsible stewards. EEN offers a regular newsletter, materials for churches seeking reflective environmental study, and the opportunity to become covenant congregations committed to the responsible stewardship of God's creation.

International Consultancy on Religion, Education, and Culture (ICOREC), The Manchester Metropolitan University, 799 Wilmslow Road, Manchester M20 8RR, UK.

The North American Conference on Christianity and Ecology, 1522 Grand Ave. #4C, Saint Paul, MN 55105. The Conference publishes *Earthkeeping News*, a newsletter with current information on conferences, legislative issues, publications, and environmental news.

Secular environmental groups

Defenders of Wildlife, 1244 19th St. NW, Washington, DC 20036. An 88,000 member organization focusing on protection of wildlife and restoring animals and plant life to natural settings.

Environmental Defense Fund, 257 Park Avenue South, New York City, NY 10010. This mainstream group with over 200,000 members litigates against polluters and government agencies. Its staff includes lawyers, economists, and scientists, and the Fund conducts an active public education program.

Greenpeace USA, 1436 U Street, NW, Washington, DC 20009. This organization of over 850,000 members is dedicated to the preservation of wildlife and natural resources, safeguarding the ozone layer, and reducing global warming. It is an action-oriented group with numerous grass-roots and global programs.

National Audubon Society, 9700 Broadway, New York City, NY 10003. The Audubon Society is making the transition to a multi-interests environmental organization from its origins as a bird conservation club. It supports wildlife refuges, manages a system of eighty sanctuaries, and helps restore threatened species. Through its local chapters and "action alerts," it monitors legislation.

National Wildlife Federation, 1460 16th St. NW, Washington, DC 20036-2266. Known for its quality publications, grass-roots and lobbying activities, the National Wildlife Federation is one of the largest and most active environmental groups. Its *Ranger Rick* magazine for children 6–12 and *Your Big Backyard* for preschoolers are particularly recommended.

The Nature Conservancy, 1815 North Lynn St., Arlington, VA 22209. This group is noted for having bought more than 3.5 million acres in fifty states since 1951. Its professional scientific staff does major work on identifying plant and animal life and working for its preservation. Local branches check research plots, search for plants, and otherwise support research activities.

Sierra Club, 730 Polk St., San Francisco, CA 94109. One of the largest and most active environmental organizations, the Sierra Club was founded in 1892 by John Muir. It has a widespread network of local clubs that track environmental issues; lobby local and national lawmakers; and sponsor hiking, backpack, and camping trips.

The Wilderness Society, 900 17th St. NW, Washington, DC 20006. Creating and preserving wilderness as a resource for humanity is one of the society's goals. Its political agenda includes preserving the ancient growth forests of the Pacific Northwest, safeguarding wildlife refuges, and following legislative proposals on the use of public lands.

United Nations sources

The World Meteorological Organization in Geneva tracks global climate change, ozone layer depletion, water levels, and related issues, including the importance of climate change to developing countries. WMO, Public Information and Press Office, 41 Giuseppe-Motta, Case postale 2300, CH-1211 Geneva 2, Switzerland.

The United Nations Environment Program works extensively with global religious leaders on ecological issues. Some of its interfaith publications include a compilation of prayers and environmental facts, *Only One Earth*, and a periodical, *Sabbath Newsletter*, with numerous ideas for young people's programs. An important scientific-public policy study is UNEP's *Caring for the Earth: a Strategy for Sustainable Living*, 1991. UNEP, 2 United Nations Plaza, Room 803, New York City, NY 10017.

On environmental and other public policy issues, church representatives are a voice to be reckoned with by government officials at all levels. Church groups should compile a list of elected and appointed representatives at the local, county, state, and national levels and should call or write them as appropriate. A brief, thoughtful letter about a specific issue is most effective. Church members need to write large corporate polluters, many of whom are even more sensitive to their public image than politicians. Track national issues through the National Wildlife Federation legislative hotline.

The author acknowledges permission to reprint excerpts from his earlier works appearing in *Episcopal Life*, the *Episcopalian*, Forward Movement Publications, the *Living Church*, and to Daniel B. Botkin to quote from a manuscript, "Ecological Theory and Natural Resources Management: Scientific Principles or Cultural Heritage?"

The publisher gratefully acknowledges permission to quote the following copyrighted material:

Excerpt from "Advice to a Prophet" in *Advice to a Prophet and Other Poems*. Copyright © 1959 and renewed 1987 by Richard Wilbur. Reprinted by permission of Harcourt Brace and Company.

Excerpts from *Carmina Gadelica* reprinted by permission of the publisher, Scottish Academic Press, Edinburgh, Scotland.

"Charm for Bewitched Land" and "Riddle #66 Creation" from *Poems from the Old English*, translated by Burton Raffel. Copyright © 1993 by Burton Raffel. Used by permission.

Excerpts from "The Days" and "The Transfiguration" by Edwin Muir from *Collected Poems*. Used by permission of Oxford University Press and Faber and Faber, Ltd.

Excerpts from "A Discussion Document on Christian Faith Concerning the Environment" in *Floods and Rainbows: A Study Guide on the Environment—for Those Who Care about the Future* (London: Methodist Church Division of Social Responsibility, 1991) Used by permission.

"Thanksgiving over the Water" excerpted from *The Baptismal Covenant I*, copyright © 1976, 1980, 1985, 1989 The United Methodist Publishing House with permission.

While every effort has been made to secure permission, we may have failed in a few cases to trace or contact the copyright holder. We apologize for any inadvertent oversight or error.